A Heathen Family Devotional

A Heathen Family Devotional

Odinism Begins at Home

Wyatt Kaldenberg

A Heathen Family Devotional

Copyright © 2011
Wyatt Kaldenberg

All rights reserved.

ISBN: 1466292822

ISBN-13: 978-1466292826

A Heathen Family Devotional

Other Books by Wyatt Kaldenberg

Odinism: The Religion of Our Germanic Ancestors In the Modern World: Essays on the Heathen Revival and the Return of the Age of the Gods

Perceived Heathenism & Odinic Prayer: A Book of Heathen Prayer and Direct Contact with Our Living Gods

Odinism In The Age of Man: The Dark Age before the Return of our Gods

Odinism: Inside the Belly of the Beast: Essays on Heathenism inside The New World Order

A Heathen Family Devotional: Odinism Begins at Home

Heathen Family Prayer for Beginners: A Collection of Odinic Prayers for Families New to Odinism

Odinism for Beginners: An Introduction to the Odinic Heathen Religion

ALSO: I make a reprint of the famous 1800s fantasy novel, The Oera Linda Book as well as an Anthology of Early Norse & Germanic Neo-Pagans: The Early Years of Asatru & Odinism

A Heathen Family Devotional

"Hail, day! Hail, sons of day!
And night and her daughter now!
Look on us here with loving eyes,
That waiting we victory win.

Hail Gods! Hail Goddesses!
Hail bountiful Earth!
Grace us both with
the gift of speech
And healing hands while we live."

SIGRDRIFUMOL: The Ballad of The Victory-Bringer

It behooves a father to be blameless if he expects his child to be.

Homer

"I greet the sword's honed edge that bites into my flesh, knowing that this courage was given me by my father."

Gisli, Gisli Sursson's Saga

Family faces are magic mirrors. Looking at people who belong to us, we see the past, present, and future.

Gail Lumet Buckley, American Journalist

Our most basic instinct is not for survival but for family. Most of us would give our own life for the survival of a family member, yet we lead our daily life too often as if we take our family for granted.

Dr. Paul Pearshall

To destroy a people, you must first sever their roots.

Alexander Solzhenitsyn

A Heathen Family Devotional

Acknowledgments

I would like to thank Dan Moll for all his helpful suggestions.

A Heathen Family Devotional

Table of Contents

Introduction   8

1	Why A Heathen Family Devotional?	11
2	The Purpose of Family Devotionals	20
3	Making Your House Kid Safe	23
4	Create a Stable Marriage	35
5	Devoting your Family to the Kingdom of Odin	38
6	The Attack on the Western Family	42
7	Don't Drink Loki's Piss!	48
8	Your Family as a Corporation	51
9	The Family is the Foundation of the Kingdom of Odin	59
10	Sunday is Outdoors Chores Day	70
11	Monday is Family Temple Day	85
12	Tuesday is Indoors Chores Day	104
13	Wednesday is Family Government Night	131
14	Thursday is Family Game Night	158
15	Friday is Family Fun Night	163

A Heathen Family Devotional

16	Saturday is Family Adventure Day	169
17	Blood Matters	178
18	The Final Thoughts	185

A Heathen Family Devotional

Introduction

"Roman religion was the religion, first of family, then of the extension of the family, the state. The family was consecrate, so, therefore, was the state. The simple ideas and rites held and practiced by the families were adjusted and enlarged, partly by new conceptions created by new needs...."

R.H. Barrow
The Romans

This is the last in a three-part trilogy dealing with Odinism's place in the Age of Man. It can be read as a stand-alone book on the importance of creating Heathen families and Odinic dynasties, or it can be read as the conclusion to the other two books, *Odinism In The Age of Man: The Dark Age before the return of our Gods* and *Odinism: Inside the Belly of the Beast: Essays on Heathenism inside The New World Order*.

The first book, *Odinism In The Age of Man*, is about the conflict between the material world and the spiritual world. The Age of Man is a corrupt and rotten place. It's spiritually dead and manned with lost people. The Age of Man is on the decline. Our multi-verse is cyclical. The death of the Age of Man will bring the Return of the Age of Our Gods.

A Heathen Family Devotional

The Age of Our Gods is a spiritual time when direct human contact with our living Gods will be more common. The death of the Age of Man is opening up a new port-hole where the bridge of light, which connects the spirit world with the world of man grows ever brighter. Once the Age of Man dies, the port-hole between the arcane and mundane will be blown wide open, and they shall seem as one.

The second book in the trilogy is *Odinism: Inside the Belly of the Beast*, which is about the wickedness inside the Age of Man.

This book, *A Heathen Family Devotion*, is the third book in the trilogy. It is about the answer to the problem. The Odinic family helps kills the Age of Man and brings the Age of Our Gods nearer. The more we pray to our living Gods the more we empower them and give light to the Rainbow Bridge. The Divine is nurtured by our devotion, our prayers, and our sacrifice.

The family is the foundation of a Heathen society. Families turn into kindreds, kindreds turn into clans, clans turn into tribes, tribes turn into nations, and nations turn into homelands. Society must be organized from the bottom up not the top down. Materialistic world views like capitalism, fascism, and communism have failed our people. The answer is not materialism, but spiritualism.

I don't have any plans in the near future to write any more about the rot of the modern world.

A Heathen Family Devotional

Perhaps years down the way, I will address the problem more. However, for now, I will be focused on the answer to the problem, our Heathen faith. I shall write more books about the family since it is the answer as well as the Odinist religion itself.

I have already written two books about the religious side of Odinism. The first is *Odinism: The Religion of Our Germanic Ancestors In the Modern World: Essays on the Heathen Revival and the Return of the Age of the Gods* and the second is *Perceived Heathenism & Odinic Prayer: A Book of Heathen Prayer and Direct Contact with Our Living Gods*. These books aren't for beginners. My next two books will be written for people who are new to Odinism. If you wish to contact me, the easiest way is just to go to my Facebook page: Wyatt Kaldenberg. I have created a Heathen contact page on Facebook that is fairly active. As of September, 10, 2011, it has had 27,849 people pass through it. I named it the *"Asatru Odinist Heathen Pagan Kindred Contact Networking and Organizing Page"* because more people can find it that way using the Facebook search engine. It's a great place to go to meet local people. Furthermore, someone gave me the *"Else Christensen (Folk Mother)"* Facebook page. They created it, got tired of running it, and asked me if I would take it over. It has had only 2,890 people look at it since it started because the title is hard to find in a F.B. search engine, and Facebook won't let me change it to something more search engine friendly. Anyway, I hope you enjoy this book about the Heathen family, the only answer to this vile world.

A Heathen Family Devotional

Chapter One

Why A Heathen Family Devotional?

"The lack of emotional security of our American young people is due, I believe, to their isolation from the larger family unit. No two people - no mere father and mother - as I have often said, are enough to provide emotional security for a child. He needs to feel himself one in a world of kinfolk, persons of variety in age and temperament, and yet allied to himself by an indissoluble bond which he cannot break if he could, for nature has welded him into it before he was born."

Pearl S. Buck
Author of The Good Earth

Our Families are Our Temples

A heathen family devotional is something I have been wanting to do for a long time. I believe Heathenism begins at home. When I first reverted to Heathenism, I didn't understand the importance of the family to the Heathen religion.

A Heathen Family Devotional

Today, I understand that Heathenism begins at home. Your family is the greatest Heathen temple you can build. To honor the Gods, have a family and dedicate them to serving the Divine.

In the 1970s up to the 1990s, the notion of national Heathen organizations was very dominant. The idea was you create this national group by getting a post office box, and from the "national headquarter" local groups would spring up.

The national organization idea has had limited success. The bad thing about national organizations is they tend to develop a "pope" mentality. The "Asatru Pope" barking out orders to his or her minions works in the short run, but most of these national groups tend to suffer palace rebellions and create endless infighting. I have come to believe that the national organizations are more trouble than they are worth. Heathenism should be organized at the family level. If families turn into kindreds, great. However, kindreds are not as important as strong Heathen families. National organizations tend to turn the people running them into jerks.

The Gods speak to each of us everyday. We don't really need a "Heathen Pope" to talk to the Gods for us when every Heathen can contact the Divine directly. Heathenism needs to be a grassroots movement starting up from the individual to the family to the kindred to the clan to the tribe to the nation to the homeland.

A Heathen Family Devotional

Instead of a national organization trying to organize everything from above, we need to build up Heathen families into great Heathen dynasties. By great Heathen dynasties, I mean we must look at the bigger picture. We must see beyond today. We must reject the hedonism and self-indulgence of Western capitalism and sacrifice ourselves in order to create large, prominent, powerful and wealthy families that maintain their wealth and power for many generations.

In pre-Christian Europe, clans were the center of government. The Roman Senate was made up of great families. These families produced impressive abilities. The famed Emperor Julius Caesar came from the exalted Julius dynasty while the Emperor Julian, the so-called Julian the Apostate, came from the Flavian dynasty. Noble households ruled the pre-Christian world. The ancient Greeks, Romans, Slavs, Celts, Germans, and Norse were all governed by majestic bloodlines. The Norse hero Beowulf was a member of the legendary House of the Wulfing. Paganism and Heathenism were both traditionally ruled by stately families.

When Christianity invaded our homeland, it saw the noble families and the clan networks that governed Europe as a threat to Papal power. The Church did everything it could to separate the people from their families. They used Biblical authority for their attacks on the family for it was Jesus himself who said he had come to put father against son. In

A Heathen Family Devotional

Pagans and Christians by Robin Lane Fox, we are told that the woman-hating Saint Paul so hated the family that he tricked his married gentile followers of Egypt into abstaining from sex. Saint Paul nearly caused the Egyptian people to become extinct.

The prophesied Second Coming of Christ came true in the body of a greasy man named Karl Marx. The followers of Marx picked up where the early Christians left off. Marxists have executed millions of families. The socialist hero, Pol Pot, used to have children march their parents out into the Killing Fields and beat them to death with sticks and shovels. Marxists in the West promote birth control pills and abortions. They endlessly attack the family unit. Leftists in public schools work diligently to turn children against their parents. They incessantly attack our people, the West, and our values.

Early Christianity was anti-family. The Germanic tribes had a cult of the family. When the Germanic tribes took over Christianity and formed the Holy Roman Empire, they changed Christianity.

Not only did the Holy Roman Empire introduce Heathen holidays like Yule and Easter to Christianity, but the Heathens also pioneered the idea that heterosexuality and the family were Christian virtues. The Germanic people didn't care for the fact that many Catholic preachers had a taste for young boys. Northern European Catholics expected their priests to be normal and married with children. This disgust of "boy lovers" led to the formation of Protestantism.

A Heathen Family Devotional

Normal heterosexual families are the foundation of Heathenism. However, we should tolerate people in the Heathen community who are harmlessly eccentric, but not those who are dangerously weird. My experience is that anyone who can't tell the difference between a person who is harmlessly eccentric and one that is dangerously weird is normally a person you shouldn't trust around kids.

We Can't Revive Heathenism Without Reviving the Family

Modern Heathenism is wrong for not focusing on the family. Heathenism isn't about drinking mead, magic spells, and costume rituals. Heathenism is about family and direct contact with our living Gods. We will not advance to the next stage until we understand this. The Eddas and Sagas are just myths and romanticized histories written by Christians, while Asatru, Odinism, Theodism, and so on are merely contemporary theologies. Conversely, the Heathen family is the bridge to the Divine. It is what matters the most.

I am an American Odinist. I am not Asatru. My ideas grew out of my experience with American Odinism. There are British and Australian schools of Odinic thought. However, they have had little to no influence on me.

According to the Wikipedia, "The term Odinism was coined by Orestes Brownson in his 1848 Letter to

A Heathen Family Devotional

Protestants. The term was re-introduced in the late 1930s by Alexander Rud Mills." However, this is untrue for two reasons. First, in the book *On Heroes, Hero-Worship and the Heroic in History* by Thomas Carlyle- Chapter 4, Lecture 4, *The Hero As Priest. Luther; Reformation: Knox; Puritanism* given on May 15, 1840, Carlyle uses the word 'Odinism".

The notes of Thomas Carlyle's speech are, *"Odinism was _Valor_; Christianism was _Humility_...."* and *"Odin with his whole mind,--he, and all _true_ Followers of Odinism. They, by their private judgment, had 'judged' --_so_. And now I venture to assert, that the exercise of private judgment, faithfully gone about, does by no means necessarily end in selfish independence, isolation; but rather ends necessarily in the opposite of that. It is not honest inquiry that makes anarchy; but it is error, insincerity, half-belief and untruth that make it."* This was eight years before the *Letter to Protestants*.

Secondly, Wikipedia is wrong with *"The term was re-introduced in the late 1930s by Alexander Rud Mills."* The Australian Odinist Osred has been doing research on Alexander Rud Mills for decades. In Osred's amazing book, *Odinism: Present, Past, and Future*, Evelyn Louisa Price, who is known as "the First Lady of Odinism", became an Odinist in the early 1920s. Evelyn Price was an Odinist before she met Alexander Rud Mills. The two met in the late 1920s when Price attended one of Mills' lectures on Odinism. So, Alexander Rud Mills and Evelyn Price met at a public Odinist meeting ten years before

A Heathen Family Devotional

Wikipedia claims Mills re-introduced the word 'Odinism'.

The word 'Asatru' has a dubious history. I have been an Odinist since the 1970s. I have asked countless people where the word 'Asatru' comes from. I usually get the answer, *"From the Sagas."* When I ask, *"Which Sagas?"*, the reply is always, *"I don't know."* I have read about Heathenism for four decades. I have never found the word 'Asatru' before the early 1970s.

Wikipedia claims that *"Asetro, a neologism coined in the context of 19th century romantic nationalism, used by Edvard Grieg in his 1870 opera Olaf Trygvason. The use of the term Ásatrú for Germanic heathenism preceding 19th century revivalist movements is therefore an anachronism."* Wikipedia is an unreliable source. However, they are inserting 'Asetro' and 'Asatru' as the same word. If so, you could declare a 1870 date for the word. Nonetheless, the modern American spelling of 'Asatru' I can't place before 1970.

When I first got into Odinism, there weren't any books written by Heathens. The greatest source for information on Heathenism from the early 1970s to the mid-1980s was Else Christensen's The Odinist newsletter. In college during the summer of 1978, a Mormon friend of mine saw an advertisement in Solider of Fortune magazine for Irv Slauson's book, *The Religion of Odin*, published by The Asatru Free Church Committee out of Red Wing, Minnesota.

A Heathen Family Devotional

The book was a mixed bag. It was mostly a collection of earlier pamphlets and articles from Asatru and Odinist groups.

The book opened up with The First Amendment to the U.S. Constitution, because in the 1970s, we had to defend our right to practice our religion. There wasn't any tolerance of polytheism back then as we have today. In the big cities like Los Angeles and San Francisco, people were more accepting of alternative religions. However, the first ten years of my Heathendom, I lived in Mormon Utah, in the cattle country of Southeastern Colorado, and in the Bible-thumping oil town of Bakersfield, California. None of these places were Heathen safe zones. With the L.A. chapter of the Odinist Fellowship, we could rent rooms openly as Odinists. In contrast, our local Wotan Kindred in Bakersfield had to hide who we were in order to rent meeting halls. I tried to buy an advertisement in the *Bakersfield Californian* announcing the existence of our local group, and I had to fight the newspaper for two years, bringing in the ACLU, and when the paper finally folded on this issue, they allowed me to buy just one small advertisement for one time only. It amazes me how much more freedom we have today.

Reading through some of the old back issues of *The Odinist*, the Nation of Odin's magazine *Thor*, the Runic Society's *At the Sacred Source of Teutonic Strength* newsletter, and the General Erich Ludendorff Society's newsletter, it becomes clear that in the 1970s all American Heathen publications believed in national organizations ruling over local chapters. There was little to no value put on the family or the local kindred.

One thing that astonished me about at least two national Asatru groups was that the founders were afraid of their local chapters. These guys wanted to start a national organization, but they were fearful of any up and coming leaders. They were worried that the local leaders were trying to dethrone them. How funny is a national leader who is terrified of his own supporters? Any local leader who flourished at organizing was expelled from the organization. A lot of problems came from leaders' insecurities. Furthermore, many people who join groups are social malcontents who aren't happy unless they have something to bitch about. No matter what you do, these people are always unhappy. National organizations are more trouble than they are worth.

Organize on the local level. However, the first step is your family.

We are in stage one of the Heathen Revival. We are just learning to walk. We will not get to stage two and learn how to run until we become like our ancestors. We must create direct contact with our living Gods and create Heathen families that are networked into bigger kindreds, clans, and tribes. Building brick and mortar temples are fine, but building a strong Heathen family is everything.

Chapter Two

The Purpose of Family Devotionals

"Call it a clan, call it a network, call it a tribe, call it a family. Whatever you call it, whoever you are, you need one."

Jane Howard,
author of Families

The purpose of family devotionals is to make your family better Heathens. Most Heathens want to be superior parents. They want a better life for their children. They want their children to be accomplished people and grow up to stand against the Age of Man.

Family devotionals can help your children to grow up to be splendid Heathens.

We live is a very negative world. Corporations are continuously promoting an unhealthy morality that

A Heathen Family Devotional

threatens the well being of our people. Public schools have a Left wing agenda. International money controls Wall Street, and Wall Street controls democracy. It is not easy being Heathen in this decaying world. It's even harder being first-rate Heathen parents.

Heathenism begins at home. For years, I thought to be a Heathen meant you honored the high holy nights and drank mead at the blottir. However, as I grew older, I realized Heathenism must be a daily devotional to our faith. A Heathen is not just something you are at a Heathen gathering a few times a year.

The family is the center of Heathendom. We live in a world that is hostile to the family. What do we do?

I believe this is the greatest challenge facing Heathenism today. Trying to create a healthy Heathen family in a society that does not value families or children is what this book is about.

Heathen family devotionals will help to make your family stronger, steadier, and healthier.

The Age of Man is the enemy of Our Gods, our people, and our homeland. Dark forces are behind the Age of Man. The Middle Earth Serpent, the Chained Wolf, Loki, Hel, the Aetan, Night Hags, Hel-Hounds, and other demonic powers are the enemies of Our Gods and Our Folk. They promote the Age of Man and work to prevent the return of the Ages of Our

A Heathen Family Devotional

Gods.

Worshipers of the enemies of Our Gods have even infiltrated Heathendom. They work to turn Our People away from the true path to our Gods.

Loki hates the Heathen family. He and his comrades plot against the family. They wish you to turn away from Odin and his Kingdom.

I believe that prayer and devotion to Our True Faith will keep Loki, his murky ilk, and the Age of Man from entering your household.

A Heathen Family Devotional

Chapter Three

Making Your House Kid Safe

"We all grow up with the weight of history on us. Our ancestors dwell in the attics of our brains as they do in the spiraling chains of knowledge hidden in every cell of our bodies."

Shirley Abbot, author of
Womenfolks: Growing Up Down South

Kids are the most important resource we have. Protect them at all cost. The first thing you need to do is to make sure only good spirits enter your home. There are many things you can do to protect your home from evil spirits.

The thing you should do first is clean your house. Good spirits are driven away by filth, while bad spirits are attracted to muck. There are people who are so dirty that they drive away their own House Wights and Kin-Fetches. These spirits are assigned by Frigga to protect your house and your family. How disgraceful to drive away your own ancestral guardians just because you are a pig.

Furthermore, noble deeds and honor attract good spirits, while ignoble deeds and dishonor draw bad spirits. Be clean. Be noble. Good luck will come your way. If not in this lifetime, then in the next.

Two things my father did around my childhood home seem to be old Germanic traditions. The first is horseshoes over doorways or on the door itself, and the second is human shoes inside the walls. There are two schools of thought with horseshoes. One is to nail them on your front door with the back of the shoe pointing up (the two arms) so it looks like a cup. It is thought by some that the cup positioned horseshore holds the luck of the house or building. The second school of thought believes the horseshoe shouldn't be nailed to the door, but above the doorway. It can be positioned as an upright cup to hold the luck or positioned as a down turned cup (the two arms pointing down) that pours the luck all over who ever enters the house. I feel if the horseshoe is nailed on the door that the two arms should be pointing up to form a cup that holds the luck of the household, the two arms should be pointing down if it is nailed above the doorway in order to pour the luck onto whoever enters or leaves the house. I think it is important to

A Heathen Family Devotional

have the luck of the house pour on you as you leave to the outside world. It's a blessing to be washed in the luck of the house when you venture out into the cruel world.

The other thing my dad did was put shoes in the walls. I grew up in an old oil field shack that my father added rooms on that he built himself. When I was about five, my dad added a livingroom to our house. I watched him while he worked on this room. One day I saw him put one pair of shoes from each of his children inside the walls above the door and the windows. I asked him why he did this, and he replied that it was for good luck.

Shoes in the wall and lucky horseshoes have one obvious thing in common: both have to be used. The more used the better. Horseshoes have to be used so the magical essence of the horse rubs off on to them. This could be the same reason the children's shoes must be well used, so the magical essence of your kids' spirits rubs off onto the shoes. The essence on the shoes will fill your home with their spirit. Aelfin are attracted to shoes. It's good to have a friendly relationship with Light Aelfin. An Aelf living inside your walls can scare off bad spirits. Children's clothing are a good offering to House Wights. It's wise to leave offerings to House Wights inside the walls.

The lucky horseshoe is a common idea throughout European cultures. The ancient Celts believed horse shoes kept out the Fair Folk and other unwanted creatures. In Celtic lore, they seem to have lots of problems with the little people. It's hard to tell whether the Celtic problem with elves and other magical creatures is a Christian addition or if the Celtic Heathens pissed them off somehow. Nonetheless, Odinism is a Germanic religion, and Germanic people have a good relationship with Aelfin and other wee people. Therefore, we don't put things above our doors, windows, and fireplaces to keep out the helpful spirits. We do it to keep out bad spirits. As Odinists, we want Aelfin, fairies (the magical kind), House Wights, Kin-Fetches, and other well-behaved spirits living inside our homes. Noble spirits hate corrupt spirits and will drive the evil out of your home. Why would anyone want to keep good spirits out of their home?   Being afraid of good spirits is a Christian thing.

Horseshoes were used as a charm against demons, witches, and witchcraft. In Germanic cultures, horses are associated with good magic and numerous Gods. Njord is a sea God associated with horses. Seamen use to nail horseshoes to ship masts in order to protect them from storms. Frey and the Vanir, in general, are associated with horses, horse magic, and horse sacrifices. Horse blood has a lot of magical properties.

Thor is a great protector. He is a killer of Aetan. He frightens the hell out of evil spirits. Thor has lots of symbols: the hammer, the swastika, the lightning bolt, the Thorn rune, the Kenaz rune, the Sig rune, the Othalaz rune, oak leaves, acorns, goats, and so on. Putting symbols of the God Thor around windows, doorways, fireplaces, or any other place evil can enter your house is a smart idea. Good spirits have nothing to fear from Thor. Bad spirits do. You can have protective symbols encircling entrances to your home, or you can have just one symbol at the top of the opening. You can put them on the outside, the inside, or in the middle.

Odin is the God of Fatherhood. He is a great protector of fathers and children. He is an enemy of Loki and other evil forces. Odin is a wonderful God to welcome into your home. Odin's symbols are the spear, the sun wheel, two ravens, two wolves, an eagle, hunting dogs (such as greyhounds used on the Wild Hunt) an eight legged horse, a single eye, the Ansuz rune, the Gebo rune, the Eihwaz rune, the Hagalaz rune, the Dagaz, the Othalaz rune, a hangman's noose, and so on.

Frigga is the Goddess of Motherhood, protector of children, and guardian of homes. Her symbols are the Berkano rune, house-keys, brooms, spinning wheels, distaffs, spiders, spider webs, falcons, clouds, house dogs (in contrast to hunting dogs) a mother holding a baby, and so on.

Frey is the God of Ancestors and King of the Light Aelfin. He watches over and protects bloodlines. His symbols are an erect penis, boars, a white stallion rampant, 12 white horses, stags, stag horns, the Fehu rune, the Uruz rune, the Wunjo rune, the Ehwaz rune, the Ingwaz rune, and so on.

A Heathen Family Devotional

Sunna or Sol is our Goddess of the Sun and Divine fire. She protects us in the daytime. She shines her light on darkness and burns it away. The sun wards off evil. Her symbols are the sun, art with a woman's face in the sun, the swastika, the sun wheel, and so on. It is helpful to have photos of the sun or art of the sun around your house to protect it from the blackness.

Mani is the God of the Moon. He shines his light during the night time and watches over us as we sleep. Mani's symbols are the moon and art with the face of the man in the moon. It is helpful to have photos of the moon or art of the moon around your house to protect it from the darkness. Actually, it's the things that hide in the darkness you really have to worry about.

Celt knots are for keeping evil out. The idea is that evil is stupid. It sees a Celtic knot and follows the lines of the knot like a road. The lines in the Celtic knots are unbroken. Therefore, the evil spirit is trapped, traveling on the neverending road of knots. This snares the evil spirits in the knot lines and prevents them from entering your home. Celtic knots and other protection symbols can be either put completely encircling your doors, windows, fireplace, and so on, or they can be put above them.

Pennsylvania Dutch hexes are both attractive and renowned for keeping bad things out of places. The so-called "evil eye" is not evil, but it is an eye that frightens off evil. Evil eyes look cool painted above your doorway. Someone once told me that the "evil eye" was actually the eye of Odin, and this is why it scares evil spirits. I don't know if that is true or not, but it sounds cool. So, what the hell?

Runes are great protection. I already mentioned the Sig or Sigil rune and the Thorn or Thurisaz rune. Other protection runes are the Berkano, the Ehwaz, the Elhaz, the Tiwaz, the Dagaz, and the Othalaz.

The Berkano rune is associated with the Goddess Frigga. She is the Goddess of the Home and protector of children. The Berkano rune means "birch tree", and birch protects against witches, witchcraft, and demons. The Ehwaz is the horse rune. Horse spirits are powerful and they often watch over people and attach to a family. The Ehwaz rune is the Elk rune. The Elwaz protects against hard times and food storages. The Tiwaz rune is the rune of the War God Tyr. He fights against evil and keeps the wolf away from your door. The Dagaz is the rune of daytime. It is associated with both the God Odin and the God Dag. It wards off the darkness. The Othalaz rune is the rune of the home. It watches over what is yours. It's the rune of home defense.

Trees are very important in Odinism. During the winter solstice and the summer solstice, the doors between Midgard (our world) and the other worlds open a crack. These cracks last a fortnight, but they are opened the most on Mother Night (Mid-Winter's

A Heathen Family Devotional

Eve) and Mid-Summer's Eve. The Celts believed the cracks opened wide on the evening of October 31st, and some Germanic tribes believed the cracks opened wide on April 30th. I believe they open at all eight of the high fire stations (both solstices, both equinoxes, and the four mid points: around February 1st or 2nd, April 30th or May 1st, near August 1st, and October 31st or November 1st). However, the two solstices are when the doors between our world and the other worlds open the widest.

During Yuletide and Mid-summer, it is smart to put garland around your windows, doorways, and fire-places in order to keep dreadful things out. Garland made of sacred trees also attracts wood spirits and other good stuff.

During Yuletide and Mid-summer, put wreaths made from scared trees on the front door of your home to let malevolent things know they are not welcome.

Many, but not all, of our sacred trees are excellent for protection. Elder trees are scared to our Goddess Holda, the guardian of souls. Elder trees ward off witches, demons, and other baneful Wights. Plant elder trees by windows, doors, or any place you wish to protect. Elder trees make terrific garland and wreaths. Birch trees ward against evil spirits. They are holy to Frigga, Bertha, and other Goddesses. Like elder trees, birch trees are fantastic for planting on areas you want protected,

A Heathen Family Devotional

and they make wonderful wreaths and garland.

Pine trees are splendid protectors of families and slayers of guilt, doubt, and self-hate. They make terrific smelling wreaths and garland. Like all sacred trees that protect, it's wise to plant them in your yard and near doors and windows.

Ash trees are a symbol of Yggdrasil, our world tree, the cosmic mother. Ash trees have a special Yule-tide and Mid-Summer connection.

Yew trees are superb for making a protective hedge around graveyards and your home. Bad things don't like walking past a yew tree. The Gods Odin and Ullr are both associated with yew trees.

Beech trees are a complex tree. They are protectors of Wyrd and luck. However, they can show people their true selves, which is not always a pleasant thing. If I ever planted a beech tree in my yard, I would keep it away from my house. Beech trees reveal hidden secrets. It's better for the general Frith or peace of a household to allow family members to keep most of their secrets. It's smart to plant beech trees in a remote area of the yard or in a sacred grove far from your house. This way you are still caring for the beech tree, it still watches over your Wyrd, and you can go to the tree and seek council from it, but it is far enough away from your home not to cause problems in everyday family life.

Adler trees are like beech trees, but more so. I

would never live anywhere that had an Alder tree nearby. I would never plant an alder in my yard, unless the yard was huge, and I could keep the damn thing away from my house. I would never kill an Alder tree. If it is too close to your house just move. Alders are meant to be worshiped. They belong in sacred groves where you can travel TO THEM and seek council, but keep the damn things away from your home. Alder trees are more powerful than beech trees in revealing your secrets. Alder trees are so truth revealing that they have a sinner side. They are an important holy tree; just keep them at a safe distance. Do you really want your family's dark secrets coming up to haunt you? Revealed secrets are an excessive way to shred apart your family. If you really want your loved one to hate you, there are less extreme ways to go at it.

Oak trees are the perfect protection tree. The oak is Thor's holiest of trees. Like all of our holy trees, every part is magical: the wood, the bark, the leaves, the acorns, and so on. Oak trees protect against lightning and ominous spirits. However, oak trees tend to attract lightning, so don't plant them too close to your house. I wouldn't hide under an oak tree during a lightning storm.

Holly is the most famous protective tree used in garland during Yule, because of the incredibly Heathen Yule song "Deck the Halls" and its opening line of "Deck the halls with boughs of Holly". I love this song. There is nothing Christian about it.

A Heathen Family Devotional

Deck the Halls

Deck the halls with boughs of holly,
Fa la la la la, la la la la.
'Tis the season to be jolly,
Fa la la la la, la la la la.
Don we now our gay apparel,
Fa la la, la la la, la la la.
Troll the ancient Yuletide carol,
Fa la la la la, la la la la.

See the blazing Yule before us,
Fa la la la la, la la la la.
Strike the harp and join the chorus.
Fa la la la la, la la la la.
Follow me in merry measure,
Fa la la, la la la, la la la.
While I tell of Yuletide treasure,
Fa la la la la, la la la la.

Fast away the old year passes,
Fa la la la la, la la la la.
Hail the new, ye lads and lasses,
Fa la la la la, la la la la.
Sing we joyous, all together,
Fa la la, la la la, la la la.
Heedless of the wind and weather,
Fa la la la la, la la la la.

Holly is a tree of death and rebirth, and it's a driver away of evil spirits. It's perfect for garland as well as

A Heathen Family Devotional

wreaths and is a stately tree to plant near your house.

The best outdoors protection tree is the Hawthorn, Thornapple, or May Bush. Evil hates this tree. However, it's not smart to bring Hawthorn trees indoors, because some useful house spirits don't like this tree. I doubt know the reason for this. Nevertheless, this is part of the tree lore. Sometimes two good things just don't get along. This is the way life goes.

The Hawthorn is holy to Thor and it has a connection with the Thorn rune. The thorn of this rune may be a representation of a thorn on a Hawthorn branch.

The Thorn rune is used to protect against Aetan and other baneful Wights. The power of the Thorn rune to protect against demons most likely comes from Thor's holy tree, the Hawthorn.

A Heathen Family Devotional

Chapter Four

Create a Stable Marriage

"Give me the life of the boy whose mother is nurse, seamstress, washerwoman, cook, teacher, angel, and saint, all in one, and whose father is guide, exemplar, and friend. No servants to come between. These are the boys who are born to the best fortune."

Andrew Carnegie
American Steel Tycoon

The most important thing you can do as a Heathen is to create a stable marriage and a loving environment for your children. I know in this society, creating a permanent marriage is not an easy thing to do. Actually, it's harder than hell, and you have to work your butt off to do it.

A Heathen Family Devotional

The popular culture doesn't support marriage, and the government is a tool of special interest groups that don't care about the well-being of our people.

Nonetheless, marriage is the foundation for a Heathen society. Our religion is family-based. Without the family, there can be no Heathendom.

The best Odinic family is made up of a Heathen father and mother. If you are a Heathen man or woman, it is hard to find a soul mate. We are a tiny minority.

However, people do find good mates. Sometimes you can go to Heathen gatherings and meet someone, or you can meet them on the Internet.

Many Odinists marry non-Heathens and try to revert them back to the "olden ways". Marrying outside our religion has mixed results. Most often, when two parents are from different religions, their children are raised with no religion at all.

Since Heathen mates are difficult to find, go out of your way to make a marriage to a Heathen partner work.

A number of Odinist men told me that they married Christian women and reverted them back to Heathenism. They claimed these Christian reverts make great wives. Well, if you can honestly bring a Christian back to Heathendom, then go for it. What works is what works. However, always put the

A Heathen Family Devotional

children first above your needs.

Children need a father and a mother. They need both a male and a female role model. Children who grew up in homes that had constantly changing father or mother figures tend to be less balanced than those who grew up in a traditional home. I know liberal democracy is endlessly attacking the traditional family, but a secure, traditional family is best.

This is not to say non-traditional families are always bad; it's just that traditional families have a better chance of creating a stable environment for children. Nevertheless, if you can make a non-traditional family work, then go for it.

Chapter Five

Devoting your Family to the Kingdom of Odin

"To put the world right in order, we must first put the nation in order; to put the nation in order, we must first put the family in order; to put the family in order, we must first cultivate our personal life; we must first set our hearts right."

Confucius

Yggdrasil is our world tree. She is the cosmic mother. She is the eight-legged horse that carries Odin between our nine worlds. She is everything and everything is she. Yggdrasil is the ash tree in which we live. She is beyond human understanding. Other people have their own world tree. She is the tree that belongs to our people.

Odin is the Alfather and the King of Our Gods. He is not the King of other people's Gods. He is only the King of Our Gods. Odin and his Kingdom have chosen our people to protect and serve. Our Gods

A Heathen Family Devotional

and Our Folk are bound together through gifting. Other people have been chosen by other Gods.

Frigga is the Almother and the Queen of Our Gods. She is not the Queen of other people's Gods. She is only the Queen of Our Gods. Frigga and her Kingdom have chosen our people to protect and serve. Our Gods and Our Folk are bound together through gifting. Other people have been chosen by other Gods.

Thor is the Albrother and the Prince of Our Gods. He is not the Prince of other people's Gods. He is only the Prince of Our Gods. Thor and his Kingdom have chosen our people to protect and serve. Our Gods and Our Folk are bound together through gifting. Other people have been chosen by other Gods.

Odin, Frigga, and Thor are the highest deities that live within Yggdrasil. Odin, Frigga, and Thor are the three main deities of the Odinic religion. Vanatru, Asatru, Theodism, Wiccatru, and so on are not part of Odinism. What they think doesn't matter to us.

The other Gods and Goddesses of Odin's Kingdom follow the three main deities of Odin, Frigga, and Thor. The lesser Gods and Goddesses of Our Holy Kingdom obey Odin, Frigga, and Thor. It is acceptable to worship the lesser Gods and Goddesses of the Kingdom of Odin, but never put them above Odin, Frigga, and Thor, nor make the lesser deities out to be equal with Odin, Frigga, and Thor because they are not equal. Many Asatru people do this, but they are not Odinists. Therefore, who cares what they do?

Odin and Frigga are the Lord and Lady of the Jarl or ruling caste. The Jarl caste protects the Kingdom and the Folk. Thor and Sif are the Lord and Lady of the Karl or the supportive caste. They support the Jarldom.

The Vanir are the most important of the lesser deities. They are the deities of the Thrall, runner, or "gofer" caste. The Thralls support the Karls and the Jarls.

Odin and Frigga were the patron God and Goddess of most noble families, except for a few nobles that were devoted to the Vanir. Most of the Norse people who settled Iceland were from the Karl and Thrall castes. They were farmers and manual labors. This is why Odin and Frigga have a secondary role in the Icelandic Sagas, and why Thor and the Vanir are so dominating.

The Eddas and the Sagas were written by Christians about their long dead ancestors who were largely devoted to Thor, Frey, and other deities of the Karl and Thrall castes. This is one reason the Eddas and Sagas do not play a big role in Odinism. Many Heathens have built almost a cult around these books. However, in Odinism the Eddas and Sagas should be treated like the writings of Homer,

A Heathen Family Devotional

Shakespeare, William Morris, Jack London, or any other non-Heathen writer who had interesting things to say and that could be used to supplement the Odinic religion. The Eddas and Sagas are no more a Heathen Bible as are the works of Plato or Edgar Allan Poe.

Below the lesser deities are the Aelfin, Norns, and other spirits, most of whom are our own ancestors or various kinds of Wights somehow connected with us.

Our own personal House Wights (house spirits) and our own home's Kin-Fetch are the least important to our Folk in general, since they belong to just one household, but as your own personal family goes, these household spirits are very essential to you and yours.

As far as this book goes, I am ranking Odin, Frigga, and Thor at the top of Yggdrasil in significance. Other patron Gods or Goddesses you may have belong somewhere in the middle. In addition, your own House Wights and Kin-Fetches are the roots of the tree.

Your own family's individual Kin-Fetch and House Wights are the most common pieces of the Great Divine you are in contact with daily, consequently, they are the most significant part of the Divine to you personally and to your family. Nonetheless, Odin, Frigga, and Thor are above all.

A Heathen Family Devotional

Chapter Six

The Attack on the Western Family

"When government was centralized and politics became national in scope, as they had to be to cope with the energies let loose by industrialism, and when public life became faceless and anonymous and society an amorphous democratic mass, the old system of paternalism (in the home and out of it) collapsed, even when its semblance survived intact. The patriarch, though he might still preside in splendor at the head of his board, had come to resemble an emissary from a government which had been silently overthrown. The mere theoretical recognition of his authority by his family could not alter the fact that the government which was the source of all his ambassadorial powers had ceased to exist."

Christopher Lasch, American author
The New Radicalism in America

A Heathen Family Devotional

The Gods want your family to succeed. They believe in your family. They know future Gods will come from your blood. Our Gods are good and they are always on our side.

Odin has an adversary named Loki. Unlike Odin, Loki does not want your family to succeed. Loki doesn't believe in your family. Loki hates the Gods, and he knows future Gods will come from your blood. Our Gods are good and they are always on our side, but the enemies of Our Gods are bad. They are always against our people.

Hel and other dark forces lead armies of demons who attack the Walls of Asgard and Our Folk daily. The armies of darkness are made up of the goddess of death and disease, Hel, the Aetan, the Midgard serpent, Fenris wolf, night hags, Hel-hounds, black norns, witches, and others. These demons and the people who worship them are the enemies of Our Gods, Our Folk, and your family.

Loki and the other enemies of Our Gods and Our Folk will fight against good in the final battles.

The Christian Eddas claim good and evil will destroy each other in the final battle. However, we as Odinists don't believe the Eddas and Sagas are our Bible. Therefore, we, Odinists, don't believe in the death of the Gods myth the Christians tried to sell us.

A Heathen Family Devotional

The Lokians have attacked our families for over a millennia. Pre-Christian Northern Europe was governed by a network of families. When Christianity invaded Northern Europe, the Church soon realized that the Germanic family stood in the way of Church power. Christianity assaulted the Germanic family, kindred, clan, and tribal structure of Northern European society. The Marxists (the New Christians) also see the family as a threat to their power and influence. Both the Left and the liberal capitalists do everything they can to assail our traditional families.

Politics is about who controls YOUR life. People who don't care about politics don't care about the future of their children and grandchildren. International money is a cancer. We must empower our families, create strong dynasties, and support family networks. Family is the only government that will save the West. Family networks helped our people survive from before the Ice Age all the way up to the baby boomers, who destroyed the family and the West.

The political systems of the so called Left, Right, and Center will not make it for our people. The family is central to Odinism, but the state sees the family as a threat to its power. The main goals of public schools are to teach children *not to be like their parents*, to reject the morality of their parents and grandparents, to be ashamed of their ancestors, and so on. Public schools are not very good at teaching children reading, writing, and arithmetic.

A Heathen Family Devotional

This is why so many students graduate from high school as well as college and know nothing but self-hate and Marxist bullshit.

Television is seen by the ruling class as a weapon to transform society. Wall Street wants to change us into something that isn't good for our people. Just look at what brain-dead cattle public schools, television, and all the other weapons of Loki turned our people into. There are political and financial reasons the system does what it does, but there are also demonic reasons. The enemies of Our Gods and Our Folk control the system.

Our future will be harder than today. These are the easy times. The affluent times. The free-enterprise system is devouring the earth's natural resources for quick profits. We live a lifestyle that can't be maintained infinitely. Sooner or later, all natural resources will run out, even fresh water and most food. Family structured government will be the only thing keeping people alive. The super state can't run without resources, but families can live off of just dried meat and animal furs, as they did throughout most of human history. I think family centered government will be the only thing to save mankind since it doesn't need much to survive other than the family. Most governments have to pay wages, hence it needs resources. Look what happened to Rome when they could no longer pay their army; they were overtaken by family-based Germanic tribes that fought out of family loyalty and didn't need wages.

A Heathen Family Devotional

I don't believe in socialism nor any other Utopian fantasy government. Socialism is where everyone struggles to be equal. This is an impossible goal because no two people are equal. Inequality is reality. Equality is fantasy.

Unlike socialism, tribalism is the struggle to survive. Equality is a fantasy for rich societies. Bad times are coming hard and fast. How to feed your friends and family will be the main concern once our natural resources disappear. How will the world survive without copper, cement, asphalt, tin, steel, oil, plastic, rubber, and so on? Even the timber industry will stop without access to non-renewable natural resources. It needs oil among other things. So called renewal resources can't be cheaply produced without using large amounts of non-renewal resources. This is a certainty. This is a major truth that will cause reality to crash down on future generations. Our present high standard of living can't be maintained forever. When earth's resources run out, our wealth will disappear.

The family is the only government that works well in both good and bad times. We can and must organize strong Heathen families in good times, so we can have a safety net in place when the bad times come.

Many young people believe in totalitarian governments because the public schools taught them the big lie that the state will save them.

A Heathen Family Devotional

Most young people are full of Marxist ideas. Most of them are too P.C. to know that this system filled their empty heads with Marxist propaganda.

However, not all young people are political soldiers of the Left: A few are National Socialists.

The National Socialist leader, Adolf Hitler, was a terrible leader who helped create the mess we are now in. The liberals use Hitler as a reason to ethnically cleanse the West of White people. Hitler is not the one we should turn to as our heroic ideal. We must trust in Our living Gods, our ancestors, and our families.

Hitler's madness made things into a mess and helped Churchill and Roosevelt handover Eastern Europe to Stalin. Hitler helped FDR empower his "Uncle Joe" Stalin.

I think American democracy is too tyrannical. I see capitalism as oppressive. I won't support communist totalitarianism nor National Socialist totalitarianism. The only government we can trust is a network of families. Family governments have worked in most nations since the start of mankind. The Saxon tribes or the Yokut Indian clan structure are better Folkish ideals than capitalism, communism, or Nazism.

The Heathen family is our best tool of surviving into the future.

A Heathen Family Devotional

Chapter Seven

Don't Drink Loki's Piss!

"Yes, he's got a father, but you can't never find him these days. He used to lay drunk with the hogs in the tanyard, but he hain't been seen in these parts for a year or more."

Adventures of Huckleberry Finn
by Mark Twain

Alcohol is Loki's piss. It will make you do stupid stuff. It will tear your family to pieces. Heathenism has an alcohol problem. Our alcohol problem starts with drinking rituals. The most popular drinking ritual is the sumbel. This is where the ritual leader fills a drinking horn with mead or some other form of alcohol, honors some deity, hero, ancestor, or whoever, takes a drink, then passes it on to the next person who does the same. I have been to sumbels that went on for hours. I have been to sumbels that caused worshipers to get arrested for DUI. I have been to sumbels where drunken

A Heathen Family Devotional

husbands flirted with single women in front of their wives and children. I have been to sumbels where fights broke out. One such fight involved knives. Intoxication causes problems. I can't think of anything good coming out of being inebriated.

Alcohol was one of the main reasons the Los Angeles chapter of the Odinist Fellowship fell apart. We started out with a large group of people, including many families, but drunkenness chased the families away. Drunkenness chased the women away. Drunkenness chased everyone away except the hardcore drunks. Who wants to be around a bunch of drunks but other drunks?

Be leery of people who center heathenism around alcohol. Odinism is a family-centered religion, not a booze-centered religion.

In my book *Perceived Heathenism and Odinic Prayer,* I devoted a chapter to Heathens I have known who have used drugs and alcohol in shamanism, but this has never worked, to my knowledge. Simple prayer will get you closer to Our Gods than drugs and alcohol.

Children are the most valuable resource heathendom has. We must protect our children at all costs. Drugs and alcohol make an unsafe environment for children. Protect your children by keeping drugs and alcohol out of your home.

My mother and father were wonderful parents. They

never drank. I have childhood friends who often told me their folks were great too as long as they weren't drinking. I am very thankful to Our Gods that my parents never had periods where they drank and became less than wonderful parents. Kids deserve great parents 24 hours a day/seven days a week. Give your children the best mother and father they can have. Don't drink Loki's piss!

Must reads!

Family Therapy of Drug Abuse and Addiction by M. Duncan Stanton

Don't Let Your Kids Kill You: A Guide for Parents of Drug and Alcohol Addicted Children by Charles Rubin

12 Stupid Things That Mess Up Recovery: Avoiding Relapse Through Self-Awareness and Right Action by Allen Berger Ph.D

Don't Let the Bastards Grind You Down: 50 Things Every Alcoholic and Addict in Early Recovery Should Know, or How to Stay Clean and Sober, Recovery from Addiction and Substance Abuse by Georgia W

Staying Sober: A Guide for Relapse Prevention by Terence T. Gorski

Everything Changes: Help for Families of Newly Recovering Addicts by Beverly Conyers

Reclaim Your Family From Addiction: How Couples and Families Recover Love and Meaning by Craig Nakken

Living Sober by AA Services

A Heathen Family Devotional

Chapter Eight

Your Family as a Corporation

"A leader is a dealer in hope."

> Napoleon Bonaparte

There is a big difference between being rich and being wealthy. Some families are loaded, and they spend their money wildly. However, the shrewd ones create wealth and keep it. By wealth, I mean transgenerational riches: funds that are passed down through generations. Foolish rich people spend their fortunes; the clever ones keep their wealth.

The American aristocracy sits on a mountain of old money.

When I lived in Del Mar Heights, an affluent area of San Diego, I met this woman who told me she married into old money. The woman said she didn't understand how real wealth worked until she divorced her husband. She was never asked to sign

A Heathen Family Devotional

a prenuptial agreement. Since California has community property laws, she assumed she was getting half this man's fortune.

The family was secretive, and she was kept away from the family business. She didn't know how much they were worth, but just by looking at all they owned, she knew they were well-heeled. They had old, dirty blood money made off slavery, child labor, and the pain of the working class. Her husband never worked. He just enjoyed life. He loved yachting, traveling, and partying. When she went to divorce court, she found out that her wealthy husband was legally penniless. The family was an official corporation. They didn't have a lawyer; they hired a law firm.

The law firm controlled the family's wealth in a trust fund. A board of directors, the legal firm itself, controlled the trust fund by following the corporate by-laws created by the family corporation. None of the family members could do anything to the trust fund without following the corporate by-laws and getting permission from the board of directors. All the money, property, stocks, bonds, and so on were owned by the corporation, not the individual family members.

All the homes she and her husband stayed in were owned by the family corporation. Her husband didn't even own his cars, jets, or boats. Every-thing but his clothing and other personal items, was owned by the corporation. The only money he got

A Heathen Family Devotional

was a small living allowance paid to him through the trust fund. On paper at least, her husband was poor. She didn't get much out of the divorce because the family corporation was rich, not her husband. How brilliant to set up a family corporation to protect the family's wealth against a divorce, lawsuits, and stupid family members.

Many rich people go broke because no one is looking out to protect their family wealth against dim-witted family members. The 1980s rapper M.C. Hammer made millions and pissed away all his money because he didn't have a family corporation to tell him, "No!" There was no board of directors protecting his family wealth, hence, M.C. Hammer is flat broke.

Odinic families, even working class families, must think of ways to create trans-generational wealth. We must not piss through our money and make other, smarter people rich. We must make our progeny wealthy. Materialism turns wealthy people into poor people just ask M.C. Hammer...it's "hammer time" at the poorhouse.

The husband's trust fund money was held in a diverse portfolio of properties, stocks, bonds, and so on. The corporate by-laws allowed no one to touch the principle of the portfolio. The allowances were paid from the profits made off the principle. Any profits family members didn't spend were added to the untouchable principle. Any properties a family member bought on their own, they could donate to

A Heathen Family Devotional

the family corporation, write it off of their taxes, turn around and live in it rent free. The system was created by the rich to work for the rich. Odinists must create wealth, so democracy can work for us instead of against us as it does against all working class people.

Do something for Odin, think of ways to make your Heathen family wealthier. If not rich, at least richer than you are today.

Even before written history, the family was always an economic unit. Ice Age man hunted and gathered in family units. All families have problems. However, as the old saying goes, blood is thicker than water. Families will often love you and help you when no one else will. They are important to survival.

Heathen society was made of family "corporations." The family hunted together and shared the feasts. They farmed and fished together. Blacksmiths taught their sons and grandsons the trade. There was no difference between family and business. This family-centered economy survived Christian feudalism and came to America as families crossed the frontier.

In the 1880s, over 80% of Americans owned some type of family business; mostly they were farmers. By the 1980s, around 20% of the American people made a living off their own companies. We have become a nation of wage slaves.

A Heathen Family Devotional

The free-enterprise system has killed the traditional family business and has empowered international corporations. Capitalism kills family businesses and turns people into wage slaves of Wall Street. Socialism kills family businesses and turns people into wage slaves of the state. Both capitalism and socialism suck. Family-run businesses are the road to freedom.

Odinism must lead our people out of wage slavery. We must promote our people to start family businesses. The Odinic religion needs a financial foundation in good times so we can build up our communities, and in bad times, it's all about survival. Our religion is Folkish, not universal. It can't survive without its chosen people.

Many decades ago, I talked to the Odinist Fellowship co-founder, Else Christensen, about an economic foundation for Odinism. She suggested people learn a trade. She told me when she was a little girl, there was a man in Denmark whose family made these wonderful dresser-drawers. They had done this for many generations, and they had built quite a name for themselves. She said the dressers were beautiful. They lasted for generations and many became family heirlooms. Today, you pay $50 or $60 for a crappy Wal-Mart dresser made from particle-boards, the drawers warp and jam in no time. Just more disposable natural resources in an economy that needs items to be quickly jettisoned to function profitably. She said that even in the Great Depression, there were some rich people who always had money to buy high quality luxury items. Focusing on special items and doing them well is a great way to secure wealth for your Heathen family. Wage slaves get laid off in depressions. Skilled craftsmen can always find a rich person to buy his goods. Wage slaves are a dime a dozen.

Public schools always push young people to go to college. They are part of the education industry. They want you to go to college to get brainwashed in Marxist dogma and to keep Marxist professors employed. Most college jobs are created with an affluent world in mind. When the economy is tanking and there are fewer people paying fewer taxes, jobs that need a college degree are a hard find. What good is an engineer in a society that can't afford to build anything? When the public teat runs dry, most college degrees are worthless. And bad times are coming. The West is de-industrializing. It will be worse than the Great Depression. It will be an incessant decline.

I don't believe the planet earth can maintain the West's high standard of living forever. To make matters worse, the whole human race wants to live like Americans. The earth wasn't made to support our consumer culture. Our civilizations are becoming so out of sync with nature that they are doomed to collapse.

A Mad Max future is not as far off as most people think.

A Heathen Family Devotional

Odinists must create family wealth and marketable skills. Think for a moment before choosing a career. Question the long term wisdom of going to college instead of a trade school.

Look at doctors, they go to college for a decade or more. In good times, they are paid wonderfully, but, unless you can become a private doctor for some rich people, in bad times, doctors get paid next to nothing. My father told me during the Great Depression, he got free rent because no one could afford to pay rent, and my father's landlord was happy to have my dad living there because he took good care of the place. He fixed the roof, painted the house, and so on. The landlord said he could work the rent off, and he never paid for rent. This bungalow set on a good piece of land, so my dad had animals and a huge garden.

Most doctors rely on the masses to make a living. When the common folks have no money, the average doctors are screwed. During the Great Depression, when my father needed a doctor, he paid them in fresh eggs, vegetables from his garden, or with chickens. Doctors were happy to get paid in fresh food because most people couldn't pay the doctors even with eggs, and the doctors worked for free. The masses are hit hardest in lean economies. Any job or trade that depends on the masses to have money is screwed in hard times. Always aim your trade at the rich, because even in the Dark Ages when most people were starving, the wealthy had money to spend. There will always be rich

A Heathen Family Devotional

people. Even under Communism, the leaders of the Communist Party are always rich.

Working for someone else is slavery because you are always at their mercy. As many of my fellow baby boomers are learning, when hard times hit, companies layoff older people first and rehire them (if they ever do) last. If you are self-employed, you never have to worry about age discrimination. Self-employment is more secure than working for a company.

Furthermore, no one ever got rich working for someone else. Wage slaves just make OTHER people wealth. Screw that!

Must reads!

Family Wealth--Keeping It in the Family: How Family Members and Their Advisers Preserve Human, Intellectual, and Financial Assets for Generations by James E. Hughes Jr

Family: The Compact Among Generations by James E. Hughes Jr

Preparing Heirs: Five Steps to a Successful Transition of Family Wealth and Values by Roy Williams and Vic Preisser

Wealth in Families by Charles W. Collier

The Legacy Family: The Definitive Guide to Creating a Successful Multigenerational Family by Lee Hausner and Douglas K. Freeman

A Heathen Family Devotional

Chapter Nine

The Family is the Foundation of the Kingdom of Odin

"Perhaps the greatest social service that can be rendered by anybody to this country and to mankind is to bring up a family."

George Bernard Shaw

According to the Huffington Post, "The Truth About Childless Women" by Melanie Notkin, posted July, 11, 2011, "Nearly 46 percent of American women through age 44 are childless. That's up from 35 percent in 1976." Most of these childless women are White. According to the New York Times, " Evangelicals Fear the Loss of Teenagers" by Laurie Goodstein, published October 6, 2006, Evangelical Christian leaders are alarmed that teenagers are abandoning their churches at such a high speed that only 4 percent of them will be "Bible-believing Christians as adults" this is a sharp drop down

A Heathen Family Devotional

from the 35 percent of baby-boomers and the 65 percent of the Great Depression generation.

I believe that drop in birthrates among young women and the lack of any real religious beliefs in these women are connected. Of course, there are other reasons for the sharp drop in birthrate among people, all have to do with the Age of Man: Materialism caused by the free-enterprise system. A belief in democracy (*If all people are equal, what does it matter that Whites aren't having children? The Third World is having so many that they can't feed them all. They can replace our missing children. It all equals out.*). They believe in liberalism (See Democracy). The widespread acceptance of birth control is like self-inflicted genocide, and so on. However, I believe that growing atheism among our people is the leading cause of our dying Folk. Television and public schools are two main reasons for the growth of atheism.

Most early Christians were either deranged celibates, pedophiles, or sheep herders. The reason why the Catholic Church today is full of homosexual pedophiles is that early Christianity was also led by these same people. They, like Jesus Christ and Saint Paul, were not family men nor were they heterosexuals. Family values were not central to Christianity, until the Germanic people took over Christianity and created the Holy Roman Empire. The Germanic tribes made Christianity more heathen than Christian.

A Heathen Family Devotional

Heathenism is a family-centered religion.

Sacred marriage binds husband and wife together by the authority of Odin, Frigga, and Thor. Hallowed marriage is an honor and a duty of all Heathens. Sacred marriage is the foundation of our faith and a continuation of the eternal family. The spirits of man and woman complete one another. The earthly man and earthly woman were created by Odin and his two brothers from an ash and an elm tree. Odin intends man and woman to progress through Midgard, ascend to Godhood, then return to Asgard as heavenly man and woman, recurring as part of Odin's and Frigga's eternal family.

Even before we were born on Midgard, we were members of an eternal family. Each of us are Our Heavenly Parents' spiritual son or daughter. We were put on earth to keep the bloodline of Our Gods alive.

The family is ordained by King Odin and Queen Frigga. The Heathen family is the most essential component in our multi-verse and in the eternal recurrence.

The family is the foundation of the Kingdom of Odin. Each of our families has a divine nature and a destiny to return to the celestial Kingdom.

Odin is Our Alfather. Frigga is Our Almother. We lived in Their household as part of Their family in incalculable pre-mortal lives. Together Odin and

A Heathen Family Devotional

Frigga are Our Heavenly Parents. They head the Divine Family that is devoted to Our People. Odin and Frigga created the traditional family because a two-parent family is the best environment to raise children. Single parent families are okay, but a traditional family with a father who works to bring home the bacon and a mother who stays home to take care of the kids is better. Loki and the other forces of the Age of Man endlessly attack the traditional family. Darkness does this because they are the enemies of Our Gods and Our Folk.

Our Heavenly Father and Mother love us. They sent us to Midgard to fight the seeds of Loki and to be tested and given a chance to return to Asgard as Gods. The purpose of our lives in Midgard is to weed out the weak and the inferior. We are here on earth to prove we are the chosen people of the Kingdom of Odin.

In my youth, my parents were very active in the Mormon temple. This was back in the late 1950s and early '60s. The Mormons are (or once were) a lot different than other Christians. Most Christian sects consider its members active if they go to church on Sundays. Some churches are happy if their members show up on the high holidays like Christ-mas or Easter. However, the Mormon temple expects its members to incorporate Mormonism into their everyday life.

To the Mormon church, it wasn't just the old adage, *"The family that prays together stays together."* Although, they deeply believe this, as I believe this,

A Heathen Family Devotional

to be true. Praying helps keep Heathen families together, too.

Mormons are a lot like the Jews, who so strongly incorporate Judaism into everyday life that they have Jewish doctors, Jewish actors, Jewish teachers, and even Jewish atheists think of themselves as Jewish. How many Christians think as themselves as Christian doctors, let along a Christian atheist? Most Christians today separate their religion from their daily life which is why Christianity is in such a decline.

Christians one thousand years ago didn't separate their Christianity from their daily life. They didn't just go to church. They weren't just high holiday Christians. They lived a Christian life. We, Odinists, must live Odinic lives. We can't be just high holiday Heathens.

The Mormons try to live a Mormon life. Their daily lives revolve around Mormon activities and teachings. This has helped to make the Mormon religion one of the most powerful religious sects on earth. Liberal Christian sects have always faded away with time because they are so liberal their membership melts into something else. Islam is becoming the strongest religion on earth because it demands its followers to live the Islamic life 24/7.

Our Temple pushed for Mormon parents to read to their children out of the Bible (*the Mormons used their own translation of the Bible in order to reduce*

A Heathen Family Devotional

the influence of outsiders) and Book of Mormon every night at bedtime before nightly prayers. This was a smart idea because I learned about Christianity more from my father reading to me from religious books than from going to the temple. If I didn't understand something, I was encouraged to stop my father and ask him about what the Bible or Book of Mormon meant. I was not allowed to stop the Bishop in the middle of his Sunday sermon and ask questions. Reading to our children at bedtime before nightly prayers is something Heathen families should do. However, stay away from any books written by non-Heathens about Heathenism. This means the Eddas and Sagas, too.

The problem is: what to read to our children? Heathens have no Bible...yet. This is something we will have to write or something for future generations. Odinism is not something that died in the past. Heathenism lives in the present and will live in the future as long as our people live.

No religion on earth teaches its children from mythology books. I never remember my father reading to me about Christian mythology and the Christ Myth. God was not a myth comparable to other mythological gods. God was real. Any talk of Christian mythology and Jesus as a myth was blasphemy and the creation of warped atheistic minds that Satan influenced. Any talk of Christian mythology was just atheists trying to get believers to stop believing.

Heathenism, on the other hand, wraps itself in

A Heathen Family Devotional

Norse mythology. Heathens study myths and folklore like normal religions study theology. All of these Nordic, Germanic, Anglo-Saxon, etc. myths were written down by, distorted by, and, possibly, totally created by Christians and other atheists. You can't build a lasting religion on top of a mythology of dubious origins. The Sagas and Eddas were written by Christians who thought Heathenism was false, silly, and childish. This attitude is spread across almost every page of the Eddas and Sagas. You don't have to be too smart to see they were written by people who belittled the old religion.

Heathens have a tendency to treat the Eddas and Sagas like a Heathen Bible. They teach their children about our religion from these books. This is a huge mistake. Teaching your children about Heathenism from mythology books is like teaching your children our religion is nothing but a damn myth. Myths are untrue. If you really believe our religion is a myth, and our Gods are myths, then why in the hell are you involved with it? Go, study Grimm's Fairy Tales or watch a Disney fantasy cartoon. If you really believe that Our Living Gods are no more real than Snow White and the Seven Dwarfs or Bambi, why not just stop reading books on Norse mythology and rent the movie Dumbo from Netflix?

Theology is the theory of the Divine. Mythology is the study of myths. Religions are built on theology. Cultural anthropology classes are built on mythology and folklore. Odinism is a religion, not an anthropology class.

A Heathen Family Devotional

We must write our own books about our religion from a theological point of view, not a mythological one. We need to write Heathen books for Heathen children. We need to teach our children about Our Living Gods and about Heathen theology. Leave the mythology books to Christians and other atheists.

The Church of Jesus Christ of Latter-day Saints (Mormons) is a full service church. They even have their own boy scout troops.

The Mormon church is well organized, so much so that it is more like a political party than a church. The LDS is so well organized that in less than 200 years they have made themselves the second richest religious organization in the world. They are only behind the 1,700 year old Catholic church in wealth. The Mormons push their members so hard to be successful and to have large families that Mormons now have the highest average income of any religious group. People assume the Jews are the richest, but they aren't even close to having the income of the average Mormon. This is amazing when you think Jews tend to have far fewer children than Mormons. The LDS slays the myth that big families make people poor. Lack of ambition makes people poor, not children.

In 1978, the 12th President of the Mormon Church, President Spencer W. Kimball, enacted a lot of liberal reforms that caused many old-time temple members to leave. It is a different church to the one

A Heathen Family Devotional

I went to as a kid.

The Mormon church is very different than most churches because it is so organized. The Catholic Church has a great organization among its clergy but the laity basically does nothing but goes to church and obey the church authorities. The Mormons are a network of many organizing committees, specialized activity groups, specific clergy assemblies, and so on. They hand out rule books, official guidelines, and instructions for everything. In LDS, the laity is encouraged to be part of church leadership. In fact, you aren't really considered a good Mormon unless you are an organizer of some commit-tee or church activity. They had family counseling long before it became hip and the counselors were basically one Mormon family helping another work through family problems. This is a smart idea that worked well. Every-one can afford marriage and family counseling if it is free.

With most Christian churches anyone can come in and join the church by just sitting on a pew and start singing. The Mormons made people jump through hoops to get in. There was a probation period. They would hold gathers where all the ward members met and questioned the prospective members. Then, one Sunday after the bishop finished his sermon, he would ask each prospective member and his family to stand up and introduce themselves to the ward. All the ward members were allowed to stand up one by one and ask the prospective members questions or to make a statement, pro or con, about accepting these prospects into the church. People would stand and say things like, *"My concern with the Smith family is I am not sure they understand the teachings of LDS well enough, and I am not convinced how serious their devotion will be to this church."* It was considered a privilege and an honor to join LDS. They only wanted the cream of the crop. After the prospects were interviewed by the ward, the entire ward voted on whether to allow this individual and his family to join. If I remember right, every member of the ward had to vote "Yes" in order that someone could join.

Today, I understand their membership standards are much lower.

I think the Los Angeles chapter of the Odinist Fellowship should have been stricter on who could join. We let anyone join who could walk through the door. This helped to kill our local chapter. People came with their own agendas and used the Fellowship to advance them. We had people joining simply so they could bird-dog us and cause infighting in hopes of stealing away a few members. It would have been smart to have people go through a probation period and prove they were devoted to the Fellowship and Odinism. However, hindsight is 20-20. I hope my books will help create an Odinic theology that can be used to weed out outlanders.

I read somewhere that many Germanic tribes allowed outlanders to join their group, but 100% of

A Heathen Family Devotional

the tribe had to vote "Yes." If just one tribal member voted "No," then this blocked the person from joining. This is an excellent idea. If you allow people to join your group that even one of your members has a problem with, then this problem will just grow and cause infighting and division in the group. I think that it is a smart rule that 100% of your kindred or other Heathen group membership has to vote "Yes" in order to bring in new people. Probation periods and members questioning the prospects help weed out people who don't belong.

The next seven chapters are influenced by my upbringing as a Mormon kid. Our Heathen families should be our ultimate temple. Each of our families should function as an active church.

Great books to read to your children at bedtime to teach them Odinic morality.

Aesop: The Complete Fables by Penguin Classics. This is the best collection I know of. Great for reading to kids and teaching Odinic morality.

Homer's *The Iliad* by Penguin Classics Deluxe Edition.

Homer's *The Odyssey: The Fitzgerald Translation*

Virgil's *The Aeneid* by Penguin Classics.

The Complete Brothers Grimm Fairy Tales, Deluxe Edition (Gramercy Books) by Jacob Grimm and Wilhelm Grimm

Hans Christian Andersen: The Complete Fairy Tales and Stories (Anchor Folktale Library)

A Heathen Family Devotional

Chapter Ten

Sunday is Outdoors Chores Day

"A son is better, even if born late after his father's death Memorial stones seldom stand by the road, unless raised by kinsman to kinsman."

The Havamal:72

One thing I picked up from the Mormon church is the importance of routine and assigning certain days with a particular activity. The LDS activities calendar doesn't apply to Odinism, so I created one that does.

Sunday is the day devoted to Our Sun Goddess, Sunna. The sun is outdoors, so Sunday is a great day to do outside chores. One of my fondest memories as a little kid was "helping" my father with chores. Actually, I was more in his way than anything, but he was too loving of a father to ever

A Heathen Family Devotional

let me know I was in his way. I loved "helping" him work on the car. I loved feeding the animals and watering the garden. I hated butchering the animals, but I loved the fact I could do it with my father. Outdoor work is a great father and son (or daughter) bonding time.

My parents both died around Winter Nights in 2006. Winter Nights is the last Harvest Festival in Odinism. My parents were very folksy and turned my childhood home into a " homestead." I thought it was very fitting for them both to leave with the last Harvest Festival. My mother was very sick and died first. My father told me my mother was the only woman he ever loved, and he couldn't live in a world without her. He needed to join her in the afterlife, so at my mother's funeral (which was the day most Asatru people celebrate Winter Nights) he had a heart attack and died a few days later. He loved my mother in this lifetime and into the next. How many people ever loved anyone so much that their death would cause their own? I never have. I am jealous of my father.

It was fairly common in pre-Christian Scandinavia for affluent people to hire stone masons to carve large rune stones in honor of their departed parents. A few of these rune stones have survived to this day.

Albeit there is no record of this, I imagine that less well off families would pay wood carvers to make cheaper wooden memorials, for even the poor love their parents. If your parents are or were good

A Heathen Family Devotional

people, it is noble to praise them often and publicly.

After my father died, my oldest brother was going to do the eulogy. He asked me for some stories or childhood memories I had of my father.

The first thing I recalled took place during the Vietnam war. My father was a World War II vet like many of the parents of the day. It was extremely common for fathers to tell their sons that they would disown them and kick them out of the family if they ever thought about dodging the draft and moving to Canada.

It was a hard discussion for many draftees. Many disagreed with the Vietnam war, but they didn't dodge the draft because they feared their fathers disowning them. One day out of the blue, when I was around ten years old, my father came up and told me he wanted me to know that whether I chose to go and fight in Vietnam or dodge the draft, he would always be my father and love and support me no matter what I did. I thought that was very cool. Who else's father would tell their sons they would support them if they became a draft dodger?

However, after I gave it some thought I was like *"Hey, I am ten years old. Why would my dad be talking to me about dodging the draft? Holy crap! President Johnson is shipping ten-year- olds off to Vietnam!"*

My father had given my draft dodging adventure some thought. He told me Sweden was a better

A Heathen Family Devotional

place for draft dodgers to relocate. There were more jobs, and they liked Americans. When I went to school, I was very proud my father gave me permission to dodge the draft. That was even better than a note from your mother excusing you from P.E.

I am changing the names of these people, even though they are all dead now. My father's friend Mr. Nelson had a son named Jim, who was my oldest brother's best friend. One day the government sent Jim Nelson his draft notice. Jim, like most of my brother's friends, was deeply against the Vietnam war. He wanted to tell LBJ to piss off and leave for Canada. Mr. Nelson would have none of that. Jim's father was a World War Two vet. He did his patriotic duty and served in the big one. No son of his was going to be a draft dodger. How could Mr. Nelson hold his head up high as he walked about town if his boy was a God damn yella' belly? At Jim's funeral, they had an honor guard give a twenty gun salute. They did this for all the boys who died in Vietnam. Mr. Nelson was proud of his son. He got all teary at the funeral. He said, *"Jim was a good boy. He was a patriotic American, who loved his country. Jim, my boy, he never hesitated to go to Vietnam and do his duty."* Folks comforted Mr. Nelson as he tried to hold back the tears. He held his head up high as he walked around town because his boy was an American hero. He was proud of his son's death.

A good father doesn't use his children for cannon fodder. Don't force your dreams on your children. Give them the freedom to have their own dreams

A Heathen Family Devotional

and to live their own lives.

Before my father's funeral, I told my oldest brother that if Jim had a dad like our dad, he would still be alive today and possibly Jim would have been a grandfather. What a difference a good father can make in your life.

 The second thing I remembered for my brother was when he and my second to the oldest brother wanted to work hoeing cotton. Back in the 1960s, if you were under 16 and wanted to work as farm labor, you needed at least one of your parents to accompany you. My oldest brother was 15, and my second to the oldest was 13. None of the local farmers would hire them to hoe the weeds out of the cotton rows because my dad worked in the oil fields full time. My father took his vacation early so he could go out in the damn hot sun in Maricopa Flats to chop weeds in the dirty, dusty cotton fields. I was about five at the time. My mother had a chair she would put in between the cotton rows and sit there with my newborn brother on her lap. My sister, Oleta, and I played in the dirt, while my father and two older brothers would hoe the cotton. Who in the hell would give up their vacation just so they can hoe cotton with their kids in a 110 degree dust bowl? Hell, I wouldn't. The kids are just going to have to do without a job if they think I would work my ass off doing farm labor during my vacation time. Moreover, why would my mother just sit in a damn cotton field... to be with her family? My father and mother were giving people.

A Heathen Family Devotional

To be a good parent is easy, but to be a great parent, you really have to give of yourself. My parents' children and grandchildren are all very impressed by them. They stand like a beacon in our lives. We love my parents because my parents deserved to be adorned. They earned it. I think all Odinists should work to become their children's lighthouse. An Odinic parent should be a light in the darkness. Being a great parent is a lot of hard work, but parenthood is one of the few things that everyone, even the poor, can shine at doing.

My father was proud to be working class. He often said, "A working man is a happy man." He once showed me his hands and said, "These two hands have seen a lot of hard work."

Having the hands of a working man is not something to be ashamed of: it's a badge of honor.

Both indoor and outdoor chores build moral character in children. My parents' generation were great people because, among other things, they were expected to do chores. The idea of chores started to die out in my baby-boomer generation, and they are nearly unheard of in the so called "Y" and "X" generations. Look at how the character of these generations has faded (along with family chores) from the Great Depression generation down to the greatly depressed Generation " X."

Chores help kids grow up, learn, and feel like an active, useful member of the family. Chores make kids feel important.

A Heathen Family Devotional

It's important for fathers to teach their children. This is the traditional role of the father. Before the baby-boomer generation, fathers taught their children the skills needed to survive, taught them morality, taught them religious values, and more. However, from the baby boomer's generation to today, the role of fatherhood has been besieged by the state and its creation of public schools. The father no longer is his children's teacher. The government has taken that role away from the father. Look at how screwed up America and the entire West has become since the government replaced the father as the teacher. Most problems our people have nowadays is the direct result of us allowing the state to take away our children and replace the father as the principled authority and moral compass of his children. Our children are being raised by the government. No wonder so many of them are such a fucked-up mess. Public schools are a tool of government brainwashing.

When I was three or four, my father let me go by myself into the chicken pens to gather eggs for the first time. I had entered a major rite of passage. I was no longer Wyatt the little kid, but Wyatt the mighty egg-gatherer. That's a big kid's job. Most the hen nests had only one or two eggs, then I found a hen sitting on about twenty eggs. I thought I discovered super hen from the planet Krypton. She could lay twenty eggs in a single day. I took the egg basket to our kitchen and gave it to my mother. I asked her to fry me up some egg sandwiches and went into the living room. Within seconds my

A Heathen Family Devotional

mother screamed, *"Wyatt, come in here!"* In the frying pan was a partially developed chick. My super hen was actually nesting. My mother tired to return the remaining eggs to the hen, but she rejected them and none of the eggs produced hatchlings because of me; all the unborn chicks died. I felt like crap. I learned many things from my chores that I could never have learned watching cartoons on TV. I became aware how fragile life is. I learned if you are not sure of something, ask someone for help. However, the most important thing I got out of this is the knowledge that my mistakes have the power not only to harm me, but others. My egg gathering chores taught me this at age three or four. I know people in their fifties who seem to have never learned this. Chores help your kids to mature into responsible adults. They build self-esteem and teach your kids that they belong to your family and must pull their own weight like an adult. Chores make your kid grow into better Odinists.

Many parents give their kids chores to do that are jobs the parents themselves don't want to do. The kids do the chores outdoors on a Sunday in the hot sun while dad is inside the cool house, drinking beer, and watching football on TV. My parents weren't like that. Chores meant kids got to do something WITH the folks. Chores to many kids meant they had to do crappy jobs their parents were too lazy to do. Chores in my family meant kids got to spend quality time bonding with mom or dad. Many people have bad memories of chores where they were alone, working their butts off. I have great

A Heathen Family Devotional

memories of chores where I got to harvest carrots with my father or bake bread with my mother. I think Odinists should use Sunday chores as a time to bond with your kids, talk to them, and teach them Odinic morality and values.

Fatherhood is under assault in this society. It is a revolutionary act to be the best father and husband you can be.

From before the early ice age, up to my mother and father's generation, the normal man's and woman's life revolved around the family. Family was always first. Today owning disposable consumer goods and other useless expensive crap that kills our planet is what the "normal" life revolves around.

My parents' generation weren't well-schooled. My father dropped out of the seventh grade to get a job to help support his family. This was common among his peers. However, my father was fluent in four languages. He was well-read. He read everything he could get his hands on: fiction, history, science, art, etc. Hell, once I saw him reading a book on the theories of mathematics. Who on earth would read a book on the history of math theories? I would rather go to the dentist.

Many people who were not well-schooled were a lot more educated than copious elements of our present-day college graduates. I read a collection of Civil War letters written by average soldiers to their women and families. Most of these guys were frontier farmers with little to no schooling. I was

A Heathen Family Devotional

struck by the high quality of their prose. Out on a Civil War battlefield without the help of the Internet or even a book, these poorly schooled farmers were quoting French, German, and Latin poetry and doing it accurately. A lot of these poems I never knew and had to Google just to understand what these so called "ignorant" farmers were alluding to. Without the help of a dictionary or thesaurus, they had a rich vocabulary.

Edgar Allan Poe, Jack London, and Zane Grey were all pulp fiction writers of their day. They wrote lowbrow fiction for the working class. The intellectuals of their time looked down on these authors because they lowered their prose to the limited vocabulary of the masses. Today, even university students have to have a dictionary nearby to fully understand the writings of Poe, London, Grey, and others. Back in the day, the masses didn't need a dictionary to understand these dime store novelists. University literature has to have footnotes to explain to the modern intelligentsia what even the common Latin phases in Edgar Allan Poe's writings mean. In the early 1800s, when Poe's prose were marketed to the common man, there were no footnotes explaining what the Latin meant because the common folks of the day all knew. William Shakespeare was a soap opera writer of his day. His plays were aimed at the common man which is why most of Shakespeare's plays are about the folly of the upper classes. The poor love to see how screwed up the rich really are. What is amazing about Shakespeare is the diversity of his lexis.

A Heathen Family Devotional

The other day I watched an episode of a reality show called *The Hills* that follows rich well-educated young people around as they live off their parents' money. Judging by the show, these people know less than 1,000 words.

Public schools help dumb down America. High schools often graduate people who can't read. Universities graduate people who aren't intellectual enough to question Political Correctness. The system creates public school in order to manufacture cogs for the machine. The system doesn't want free thinking people. It needs Politically Correct robots to further the system's agenda, and this is what public schools do.

Public schools produce an army of political soldiers whose job it is to protect and advance the Age of Man.

My parents' generation was well educated, but poorly schooled. The family meant everything to them. My generation, the baby boomers, were the most public schooled generation in history. My generation was taught to look down on my parents' generation and to look down on the entire history of the White race. Public schools taught my generation that the White race is evil, racist, and privileged. We were taught that White people should be ashamed of our ancestors. We were taught that Whiteness is an evil that must be overcome. We were told that we must rebel against our parents' generation and against all our ancestors.

A Heathen Family Devotional

This self-hate only applies to White people. Public schools taught non-Whites to be proud of their race and their ancestors and that the White man is the root of all of their problems. Public schools demonize White males. The system teaches that the White male is the oppressor of all. Democracy teaches that the White man is the oppressor of all non-Whites and of all women. The system has lined up everyone against the White male, even White women. Social justice is the overcoming of the evil White male. Jews were to the Third Reich what White males are to liberal democracy.

My generation was the first generation in human history to have their minds totally sculpted by public schools. My generation hated its parents, rebelled against the family, rejected tradition, denounced normalcy, questioned the system's old ways simply because the system wanted to create new ways, took harmful chemicals because capitalist pop culture told them to, obeyed the trend to become different just so they could be different like everyone else. Therefore, conforming to a new herd mentality.

My generation was the first generation to be taken away from their parents at age five and put into a government programming system until they were eighteen. The government graded these kidnapped children. The kids who sat up in the front rows and kissed their teachers' Marxist asses were given "As" as a reward for accepting government programming. The kids who were free-thinkers, rebelled against the state, and sat in the back rows were given "Fs"

A Heathen Family Devotional

for not listening to state propaganda. The students who were too weak to think for themselves got lots of "As" and were pushed into universities where Marxist professors programmed them even more with Politically Correct thoughts. The truly weak minded were moved up into the universities where they could be programmed to be obedient servants of the New World Order.

My generation destroyed the traditional family with their selfish individualism, and its slavish devotion to the false utopia Wall Street created in order to control the masses. My generation is a puppet manipulated by the Age of Man. My parents' generation sacrificed everything for their children. They created a better life for their kids who were brainwashed by public schools to rebel against their parents. The biggest mistake my parents' generation made was sending their children to public schools. This led to the downfall of America and the entire West.

Odinists should educating their own children and keep them out of public schools.

Take the television out of your house. It's a weapon of the system used against our people. Teach your kids the importance of reading. If your kids learn to love reading, then they can teach themselves.

Television and public schools reduce fatherhood to just some guy who pays the bills.

Sunday is a great day to devote to fatherliness.

A Heathen Family Devotional

Many dads work Monday through Friday and have Sunday off. Dads can use Sundays as a day to focus on their role as father. Paternity is a 24/7 job, but by focusing on being a dad for a whole day gives you a reason to define what fatherhood means. It's easy to forget about your role as a parent and pawn everything off on mom. My reason for reserving Sundays for fatherhood activities is that having a routine forces you to develop your role as dad, and it will make you a better father the other six days of the week.

Here is a prayer of thanks for Sunday chores.

"Hail Odin, the Divine Father. Hail Frigga, the Divine Mother.

I wish to give thanks for this time I am allowed to spend with my family.

Hail Thor, Lord of Skilled Labor. Hail Frey, Lord of Unskilled Labor.

I wish to give thanks for your allowing me this chance to work.

Hail Sunna, Spirit of the Sun.

I wish to give thanks for your lighting the world in order that I can work.

Hail Eartha, the Earth Mother.

I wish to give thanks for your giving me the earth to

A Heathen Family Devotional

work.

Hail the Land Wights, the Spirits of the Soil.

I wish to give thanks that you are alive and well in my soil.

Hail all that is Divine.

I give thanks for all the help you give both known and unknown.

As thanks, I make this small offering of (name the offering).

Hail all.

> *Alu, Alu, Alu.*
> *Alu, Alu, Alu.*
> *Alu, Alu, Alu.*

A Heathen Family Devotional

Chapter Eleven

Monday is Family Temple Day

"It is the logic of consumerism that undermines the values of loyalty and permanence and promotes a different set of values that is destructive of family life."
Christopher Lasch
The Culture of Narcissism

I am not a reconstructionist Heathen.

Reconstructionists want to rebuild the Heathen past. Even if you could, which I think is impossible, why would you want to bring back the past? The Anglo-Saxons failed to defend our Gods against the Christian invasion. Franks failed to defend our Gods against the Christian invasion. The Germanic tribes failed to defend our Gods against the Christian invasion. The Frisians failed to defend our Gods against the Christian invasion. The Scandinavians failed to defend our Gods against the Christian invasion. The Icelanders failed to defend our Gods against the Christian invasion. They all failed

A Heathen Family Devotional

to defend our Gods against the Christian invasion.

Why would anyone want to repeat their mistakes? They lost the way. We must find the way in our own time and return our Folk to the Age of the Gods.

Modern Heathens must build a modern religion to serve our living Gods. We must study what works today and do it. Study the Christians. Study the Jews. Study the Muslims. Study the Hindus. Study the capitalists. Study the communists. Study the fascists. Study the anarchists. Study the Tea Partiers. Study everything in the modern world that has worked or that failed and learn from it in order to build a new Heathenism.

What do people who got their asses kicked by Christians and turned their backs on our living Gods have to teach us about serving our Gods? They failed our Gods. They are not role models. They are a disgrace. You are hard-pressed to find a true hero from the past. Few stood up for our Gods. Witikind fought against Charlemagne for many decades, but he too converted to Christianity in the end.

Who wants to copy failure from 1,000 years ago?

The Christians won. We must study why they won and copy their methods. The only thing we can learn from the Heathen past is what not to do. If the ancient heathens did it, we must ask ourselves: "Is this the reason they were defeated by the Christians?" We need to create a totally modern theology that can work today to deliver us out of this Age of Man and into a new Age of the Gods.

I value studying Christianity more than I do the Eddas or Sagas. We must see how other religions operate and copy what they do that succeeds while rejecting what they do that fails. The old heathenism folded like a prison bitch to Christianity. It is not the way to our Gods. Our Gods live today. Be here now.

Monday night was left open in LDS. No church activities were to be scheduled on Mondays because families were supposed to deal with their own spiritual needs together. I think it is a smart idea to leave Monday nights open for your family's spiritual needs. Mondays are basically a dead night. If you are a true traditionalist, you won't have a damn TV in your house, so your kids won't be missing anything on the boob tube.

Television is the great corruptor of children. You want to turn your children against everything you believe, then send them to public schools and put a television in your home. TV and public schools are the two biggest mistakes of any parent.

Television promotes consumerism. It teaches your kids to want crap they don't need just because they saw it on TV. Sending your kids to public schools doesn't just fill their empty heads with system propaganda. Other people's children, who attend public schools, too, will continuously mock your kids for not owning the latest technology or wearing *"this*

A Heathen Family Devotional

year's cool clothing."

Consumerism just makes Loki's seeds rich and working-class people poor. Consumerism fuels this system and it will kill your family and the entire earth. Consumerism is more addictive than crack cocaine.

You need to own more worthless shit just like you need an arm full of black tar heroin. The key to a successful Odinic family is keeping out of the system's agenda. Use the system, but don't be used by it.

America is an idea defined by a poisonous atmosphere of propaganda. It's hard to breathe in such smog. The only way to get fresh air to a young mind is to create an environment where children can breathe freely.

The Odinic family should operate as a corporate family of one or more fathers, one or more mothers, and their children. The wealth of the nation should be distributed through the corporate family. The kindred is a multi-generational extended family. The economic center of an Odinic society must be focused on the family and not on the state as under socialism nor on Wall Street and international capitalism as under a free-enterprise system. The Folk way is to promote the family over the individual. The Family must own property, not the individual nor the state.

On Monday nights, the Mormon church encouraged

A Heathen Family Devotional

families to study Christian and Mormon literature together. The LDS was extensive in providing literature and guidelines for EVERY aspect of Mormonism. This is something Odinism must do. People can become better leaders when they have instructions and know how to do things. Parents are the leaders of their household.

We have to learn to lead our families, for if we can't even lead our families, how will we ever lead our communities?

Monday nights are a great time to teach yourself how to lead your family and how to teach your kids about morality and about our Odinic religion. Leadership is something you learn through practice. The father and the mother are the heads of the household. If you never take an active role in shaping the minds of your children, then someone else will. Look at how lost this generation is because they were raised with public schools being their father and television being their mother. How different would America be if this current generation would have been led by their fathers and mothers instead of by government-run schools and the electric toilet?

How different would Black Americans be if the family and fatherhood would have survived in their communities? Street and prison gangs operate as extended families. If the American family would have survived in poor neighborhoods, would the crime rate be as high? I grew up on an oil lease with lower-income families. Crime was mainly kids

A Heathen Family Devotional

stealing figs off of the fig tree in Mrs. Johnson's front yard. Liberals always say poverty causes crime, but we were poor and crime free. I believe that strong families and religious belief kept my childhood village crime free, safe, and a kid's paradise.

Monday nights should be devoted to you building the moral character of your kids. You must become the principled authority and moral compass in your children's lives. If not, then the system will take over your role as father or mother. You will become just someone who pays the bills as the New World Order programs your children.

Good family activities for Monday nights are:

Teach your kids the Nine Noble Virtues. In the 1970s, John Gibbs-Bailey and John Yeowell originally wrote the Nine Noble Virtues for the British organization, the Odinic Rite. Over the years, many Heathens have altered the Nine Noble Virtues to fit their own needs. Few ever give John Gibbs-Bailey and John Yeowell credit for creating the Nine Noble Virtues. Here is the original Odinic Rite's list: 1. Courage, 2. Truth, 3. Honor, 4. Fidelity, 5. Discipline, 6. Hospitality, 7. Self Reliance, 8. Industriousness, 9. Perseverance.

In the early 1980s, Stephen A. McNallen of the now dispersed Asatru Free Assembly was the first person whom I am aware of to alter the Nine Noble Virtues. Here is McNallen's version: 1. Strength is better than weakness, 2. Courage is better than cowardice,

A Heathen Family Devotional

3. Joy is better than guilt, 4. Honor is better than dishonor, 5. Freedom is better than slavery, 6. Kinship is better than alienation, 7. Realism is better than dogmatism, 8. Vigor is better than lifelessness, 9. Ancestry is better than universalism.

When Sean and I were running the Heathen Folk Revival, I wrote the 24 Points of the Heathen Folk Revival. With Point Number 13, I took some of the qualities from both the original Odinic Rite Nine Noble Virtues and the Asatru Free Assembly reformed edition and created our own version. The only original thing I added was the virtue of duty. The Heathen Folk Revival adaptation of the Nine Noble Virtues is: 1. Courage, 2. Truth, 3. Honor, 4. Duty, 5. Hospitality, 6. Ancestry, 7. Industriousness, 8. Kinship, and 9. Fidelity.

When your kids are too young to read for themselves, read to them from your favorite books. These books don't have to directly tied into Odinism. They just have to be books you can use to teach moral lessons.

Some of my favorite books as a young kid were the Curious George series, Mother Goose Nurse Rhymes, Grimm's Fairy Tales, Hans Christian Andersen's Fairy Tales, Aesop's Fables, and so on. They are short books or have many short stories. All these, except for Curious George, teach morality. These fairy tales and fables are great for teaching kids morality because this is what they were written for. Try to tie them into the Nine Noble Virtues as much as you can. Talk about the meaning of these tales and how they apply to the Odinic religion.

With Aesop's Fables, Hans Christian Andersen's Fairy Tales, and so on, you can just go online at http://aesopfables.com/ and listen to the audio with your kids or, better yet, print out text copies of many of these tales and read them to your children. I always treasured my father and mother reading stories to me more than listening to record-ings of someone else reading. It creates a family bond. After reading to your kids, talk to them about how the story ties into Odinism. Does the moral of the story agree with our Odinic world view or is the story in conflict with Odinism?

Here is an example:

The Eagle and the Arrow

An Eagle was soaring through the air when suddenly it heard the whizz of an Arrow, and felt itself wounded to death. Slowly it fluttered down to the earth, with its life-blood pouring out of it. Looking down upon the Arrow with which it had been pierced, it found that the shaft of the Arrow had been feathered with one of its own plumes. "Alas!" it cried, as it died, *"We often give our enemies the means for our own destruction."*

This is a real teaching moment. Keep a journal that helps you collect your thoughts. Write down examples in the news, history, or, even better, your own life where the moral of this story can be shown. Give your children examples of how *"We often give our*

A Heathen Family Devotional

enemies the means for our own destruction." Current news items and world history are interesting ways to teach your children Odinic values.

Real events are far better at teaching kids about our Odinic religion than myths are. This works with adults, too.

What was it that the communist leader Lenin said? In the end, the capitalists will sell us the rope in which we will hang them with. We should be careful not to empower the people who hate us.

Another example of this is my father's best friend worked for Shell Oil on the Midway Sunset oilfield west of Bakersfield, California. He had a son fighting in Vietnam. The U.S. government put an oil embargo on any U.S. oil being shipped to North Vietnam. Shell would move oil from the Midway-Sunset down to Long Beach Harbor and put it on tankers headed for Japan. Once the oil tankers reached Japan, their cargo would be transferred to ships flying the Dutch flags. The Netherlands didn't have an oil embargo against the Communist government of North Vietnam. So, the Dutch oil tankers would ship the Midway-Sunset oil from Japan to North Vietnam where the Communists would use the oil in their war efforts against the United States. How insulting would it be if oil from where my dad's best friend worked was used to grease the gun that blew his son's fucking head off? *"We often give our enemies the means for our own destruction."* In this case, our enemy is more Shell Oil than the North

A Heathen Family Devotional

Vietnamese Communists.

Here's another example:

The Ass, the Fox, and the Lion

The Ass and the Fox, having entered into partnership together for their mutual protection, went out into the forest to hunt. They had not proceeded far when they met a Lion. The Fox, seeing imminent danger, approached the Lion and promised to contrive for him the capture of the Ass if the Lion would pledge his word not to harm the Fox. Then, upon assuring the Ass that he would not be injured, the Fox led him to a deep pit and arranged that he should fall into it. The Lion, seeing that the Ass was secured, immediately clutched the Fox, and attacked the Ass at his leisure. Never trust your enemy

This is an easy one. History is full of instances where people have lost everything by trusting their enemies. Giving Wall Street the freedom to control our economy is transforming the West into the Third World. Wall Street is selling America to Communist China and to oil producing Islamic nations. Working-class people are insane to trust international capitalists. Like I said, it's easy to come up with examples of our people being harmed by trusting our enemies.

Here is the last example of an Aesop Fable:

The Nurse and the Wolf

"Be quiet now," said an old Nurse to a child sitting on her

A Heathen Family Devotional

lap. *"If you make that noise again I will throw you to the Wolf."* Now it chanced that a Wolf was passing close under the window as this was said. So he crouched down by the side of the house and waited. *"I am in good luck today,"* thought he. *"It is sure to cry soon, and a daintier morsel I haven't had for many a long day."* So he waited, and he waited, and he waited, till at last the child began to cry, and the Wolf came forward before the window, and looked up to the Nurse, wagging his tail. But all the Nurse did was to shut down the window and call for help, and the dogs of the house came rushing out. *"Ah,"* said the Wolf as he galloped away, *"Enemies promises were made to be broken."*

As a kid, the spookier fables and fairy tales always had a more lasting impression on me.

When I grew older, my favorite books were H.G. Wells' *War of the World,* the *Red Badge of Courage, Treasure Island,* the *Adventures of Huckleberry Finn,* and so on. When your kids get older, you can read these books with them, perhaps doing a chapter or two each Monday night. Read the books first and search them for any examples of how they relate to our Nine Noble Virtues or some other aspect of Odinism. Talk to your kids about the books and Odinism. Everything in our multi-verse relates to Odinism.

You can also watch a movie and talk about how it applies to our religion. Are there good and bad people in the movie? What makes them good or bad? What lessons does the movie teach? Watch the movie first so you can tell whether or not it can be a

A Heathen Family Devotional

good teaching tool, and you can take notes and look for things that relate to Odinism.

Odinism is a religion. The worse thing any Heathen can do is to turn to non-Heathen sources and allow them to con us into turning our religion into a mythology. Myths are not true. Religion is true. Would a Christian, a Jew, or a Muslim teach their kids about the "myths" of their religion? Using books on Norse Mythology, the Sagas, and Eddas lowers our Gods down to the status of Santa Claus, the Easter Bunny, Cinderella, the Cat-in-the-Hat, as well as Paul Bunyan and his Blue Ox, Babe.

If you turn our Gods into a mythology, they might believe in them when they are very young, as they do the Tooth Fairy or Santa, but as they get older, around eight or nine, they will stop believing in Norse myths as they will stop believing in Santa Claus. It's suicide for Heathenism to keep seeing our religion as a mythology. No one believes in myths. Ancient Heathens didn't believe that their religion was a bunch of myths. The ones who did quickly converted to Christianity in order to join a real religion. Who would devote their lives to myths? People devote their lives to truths.

American Odinism goes back to 1964, when Alec and Else Christensen discovered it. I have heard stories that the Australian Odinist, Alexander Rud Mills had American followers back as far as the 1920s or 1930s. The only proof of that is in the early 1980s someone gave me two of A. Rud Mills' poetry books that belonged to his late father, so at

A Heathen Family Devotional

least Mills' books made it to America. However, I don't know when his father got these books, and if he was an Odinist or not. Our modern-day Odinist religion is the only part of Heathenism we can study that is free of Christian and other non-Heathen influences.

Recently, in America, there was a famous murder trial of a woman named Casey Anthony for the murder of her little girl. Casey Anthony is a psychopathic liar. Casey's mother, the murdered girl's grandmother, Cindy Anthony, is a liar. The whole family is a bunch of liars. They live in a mythological world.

In the 1600s, during a Witch Trial, a Christian testified in open court that a cow flew up into a second-story window and had sex with a woman, a witch, who was sleeping in her bed. Cows are female cattle. A bull is a male cattle. So this Christian testified that a female cow flew like a bird up into this witch's bedroom and had inter-species lesbian sex with a human woman. The Christian was outside the home, so I have no idea how she saw this other woman and a cow having lesbian sex in a second-story bedroom, but this was her court testimony. Read about the Witch Trials. Christians swore to their god to tell the truth, and they testified to some of the craziest shit ever testified to in a court of law. Christians have a long history of lying about anything and everything related to non-Christians. Christians testified in court that Jews kidnapped Christian children, sacrificed them, dipped bread into their blood, and ate it for

A Heathen Family Devotional

Passover. Christians are totally full of shit when it comes to non-Christians. In and around the 1300s, Icelandic Christians wrote the Sagas and the Eddas. No ancient heathen ever even heard of the Sagas and Eddas because they were not created until after the passing of the Heathen Age. Too many modern heathens treat the Eddas and Sagas as a Heathen Bible. They are not. They are not even Heathen. They are Christian. To believe what a Christian wrote about Heathenism is like asking Casey Anthony, "Who murdered your daughter?" She is a psychopathic liar. The only thing you'll get from her is bullshit. The same thing you'll get from a Christian writing about Heathenism.

The only things about Heathenism we can trust are things given to us by Heathens. The only written sources composed by Heathens are by modern-day Heathens. Odinism is a living religion. It is not trapped in old books written by Christians. It is here and now. The only Heathenism that has survived is the Heathenism today. The Eddas and Sagas can be a good resource if you understand they are Christian bullshit and treat them that way, but don't ever use them as a teaching guide for your children because they will mislead them.

The only way real heathen books will exist is if modern-day Heathens write them.

It is crucial to teach your children that Odinism is a modern religion that is significant today. Too many Heathens treat our religion like it is a dead religion that lived long ago. We can't act like Heathenism is

A Heathen Family Devotional

something that was. It's the religion of now.

Our Gods live today. We can make direct contact with them today. Why do books on Norse mythology written by non-Heathens about what Christians wrote about us matter to a living Heathen religion? Screw outlanders! We can't allow them to define our religion. Our Gods speak to each of us every day. Listen to our Gods, not to the outlanders. Our Gods will teach us about Heathenism.

Keep a religious journal. It helps you to know what you covered in your lessons to your kids. The journal will help you organize family study. Furthermore, write down what bores your kids in addition to what keeps their interest. Most kids are different. It pays to keep a record of their reaction to your teaching methods. The worst thing an Odinic parent can do is make Odinism boring.

As a child, I loved my parents teaching me about Mormonism, but one thing I hated was the first or second, I forget which, Monday of the month, Mormon Ward teachers would come to our house, meet with our family, and talk to us for what seemed like hours about Mormonism. Unlike my parents, the Ward teachers bored the hell out of me.

Once when I was about five, I was out in the front yard watering the grass when suddenly I heard this creepy music from the Wizard of Oz. You know the music they played when wicked miss Almira Gulch gets a court order to acquire Dorothy's dog, Toto, and have it put to sleep? When the old witch is

A Heathen Family Devotional

riding her bike the music goes: "Dunt-ta-da-ta-da-da-dunt-ta-da-ta-da-da-dunt-ta-da-ta-da-dadunt-ta-da-ta-da-da-dunt-ta-da-ta-da-da...."

Well, I looked down the street. In the distance, I could see two men on ten speed bicycles. They wore shiny black FBI shoes, black dress pants, a white dress shirt, a black tie, their hair was greased back, each was carrying a book pack on their backs, and they were making a bee-line to my house. I thought this is Monday evening. *"Jesus Fucking Christ, it's the Mormons!"* I threw down the water hose without turning it off and, like a "Jack Mormon" Paul Revere, I cried, *"The Ward teachers are coming!"* as I ran up the stairs into the house. My mother grabbed me and said, *"I am not sitting through this by myself.,"* and she sat me down on the sofa where I had to sit like a good little Mormon boy, with my hands neatly folded, and listen to THEM talk. Making me listen to Ward teachers lecturing me was the closest to child abuse my parents ever got.

Mormon Ward teachers are more boring than the Jehovah's Witnesses, and the Witnesses are as tedious as listening to milk sour.

At first, the entire family would stay in the living room and listen to the Ward teachers, until one day my father had enough, and every time they came, he would run and hide in the kitchen. He would abandon my mother and his five kids in that living room with THOSE PEOPLE. Finally, one day my father asked us why we all didn't join him hiding in the kitchen. All us kids were joyous that we had

A Heathen Family Devotional

father's permission to hide in the kitchen, but my mother would have none of that. She thought it was rude to run from people who only wanted to talk to us about the good Lord.

The next time the Ward teachers came around, they knocked on the front door, my dad peeked out the window, and bolted for the kitchen. We kids realized this was our opportunity to make our great escape. Suddenly, a large crashing sound could be heard as kids tripped over coffee tables, knocked over lamps, chairs flew everywhere as the Kaldenberg brood made a mad dash for the safety of our kitchen. We were loud. All this time the Ward teachers standing outside the door could hear everything going on.

My mother, like a trooper, braved it out and let them inside. She sat there by herself listening to them. They knew we were hiding in the kitchen, but they asked my mother, *"Where's Philip and the kids?"* She just stammered. Once and a while, I'd open the kitchen door and look out to see if the coast was clear, then called back, *" No, they are still here."* I said it loud enough so they could hear me. Afterwards, my mother was furious. She said that was the most embarrassing thing she ever went through. If she had to sit and listen to those boring people, then the whole family should. Each month after that we did the same thing. Every night the Ward teachers showed up, we all ran, hid, and left my mother there to take the punishment by herself. Luckily for my mom, the Ward teachers got the message no one wanted to talk to them, so they just stopped coming around. The Lord works in

A Heathen Family Devotional

mysterious ways.

Odinism should never be that boring. The fastest way to lose kids is to bore them. I have seen too many Heathen meetings that were focused on adults. Kids were never given any thought. Drunken rituals are not kid friendly. What mother would want her children around a bunch of drunks?

Kids are the future. Focus on them and families will be attracted to your group. Focus on drunkenness and drunks will be attracted to you.

Monday nights are a way of turning your family into a kindred. Do the Monday Family Temple nights. Teach your kids. Tell other Heathens about it. One Monday night a month, invite a few local Heathens to meet you in a public place like a pizza joint. If they seem like normal people, have religious services with them one Monday a month. Save the other Mondays for your family. If you get along with these people, keep the first Monday open to meet with them. This way, your family can meet with other Heathens. Slowly, you can build up a local kindred. If everything seems to work, great. However, if you have any problems with local Heathens, just stop meeting with them. They don't know where you live, so if they are bad news you never have to see them again. You may want to give them a fake name at first until you get to know them better.

Here's a closing thought about teaching your kids about Odinism:

A Heathen Family Devotional

The biggest problem with Norse myths is all of them were recorded, re-written, or totally made up by Christians 200 years AFTER Heathendom. There's a huge chance that the myths in the Eddas, Sagas, etc. would be unknown or at the very least different from what the Heathens knew. We don't even know if these are Heathen Norse myths or Christian Norse myths about Heathenism.

The Gods are here and now. Pray to them, talk to them. The Gods are living beings. You don't need to study the past to find something that is here and now.

Here is an easy prayer you can teach your kids. This is a children's prayer, so I'll repeat words so they can remember it more quickly.

"Hail Odin, our heavenly father. Hail Frigga, our heavenly mother. Hail Thor, our heavenly brother. Hail all that is Divine.

I thank you for all the things you have blessed me with.

Please accept the gift of my love and devotion.

Alu, Alu, Alu.
Alu, Alu, Alu.
Alu, Alu, Alu.

A Heathen Family Devotional

Chapter Twelve

Tuesday is Indoors Chores Day

"No ordinary work done by a man is either as hard or as responsible as the work of a woman who is bringing up a family of small children; for upon her time and strength demands are made not only every hour of the day but often every hour of the night."

U.S. President Theodore Roosevelt

"The principal cause of boredom is the hatred of work. People are trained from childhood to hate it. Parents often feel guilty about making children do anything but the merest gestures toward work. Perhaps the children are required to make their beds and, in a feeble and half-hearted fashion, tidy up their rooms once a month or so. But take full responsibility to clear the table, load the dishwasher, scrub the pots, wipe the counters? How many have the courage to ask this of a ten-year-old? It would be too much to ask of many ten-year-olds because parents have seriously asked nothing of them when they were two or three. Children quickly pick up the

A Heathen Family Devotional

parents' negative attitudes toward work and think of it as something most sedulously to be avoided."

Elisabeth Elliot
American romance writer

"Metrosexual man, the single young man with a high disposable income, living or working in the city (because that's where all the best shops are), is perhaps the most promising consumer market of the decade. In the Eighties he was only to be found inside fashion magazines such as GQ, in television advertisements for Levi's jeans or in gay bars. In the Nineties, he's everywhere and he's going shopping."... "For some time now, old-fashioned (re)productive, repressed, unmoisturized heterosexuality has been given the pink slip by consumer capitalism. The stoic, self-denying, modest straight male didn't shop enough (his role was to earn money for his wife to spend), and so he had to be replaced by a new kind of man, one less certain of his identity and much more interested in his image – that's to say, one who was much more interested in being looked at (because that's the only way you can be certain you actually exist). A man, in other words, who is an advertiser's walking wet dream."

Mark Simpson
British journalist

In this culture, most marriages end in divorce. Most children come from broken homes. Liberal democracy has not been good for our people.

A Heathen Family Devotional

Capitalism has changed Western traditions for the worse. Over 60 years of consumerism has caused the decline in the traditional family and in morality.

This culture kills communities, alienates people, and turns them into simple consumer units.

All humans need a father and a mother. People who don't have both fill the gap somehow. Some people fill the gap of a missing parent with evil people.

Single parents can raise great kids, but the human mind will always replace a missing father or mother. Not all people, but many people from single households replace the missing parent with bad people. Many dysfunctional teenagers habitually switch their absent father with a dark substitute father like Satan, Varg, Vlad the Impaler, Jeffrey Dahmer, Charles Manson, John Wayne Gacy, Hitler, Mao, Che or countless other villains from history or the daily news. The biological father abandoned them, and they see him as evil. These people go into Wal-Mart and see a t-shirt with Che's face on it. They think, *"Che was Fidel Castro's executioner. He personally murdered thousands of innocent men, women, and children. My father left me. My father is evil, but Che was much worse than dad. Evil equals fatherly love. Che could be my super dad. I am buying this t-shirt. Thanks, Wal-Mart, you gave me a father!"*

One of the first things all totalitarian states do is try to break up the family. The Catholic church did this

A Heathen Family Devotional

in the Dark Ages. It took children away from their Heathen parents and "educated" them in the teachings of Christianity. The Third Reich did this when it took children away from their parents and "educated" them in the teachings of National Socialism. The Communists did this when they took children away from their parents and "educated" them in the teachings of Marxism. Now, this system is doing it when they take children away from their parents and "educate" them in the teachings of liberalism and consumerism.

The family always stands in the way of the state. Dysfunctional families mean the state becomes your father.

I keep noticing how many young people worship totalitarian cults. They worship mass murderers like Che, Mao, Lenin, Trotsky, Hitler, and Pol Pot. Most of these cultist come from fatherless or dysfunctional homes. Their fantasy relationships with totalitarian idols are the closest thing to a father these people ever had. The breaking up of the family is making totalitarianism more popular. Whenever a moron wears a Che t-shirt, it's really the face of dad.

What cracks me up about these totalitarian cultists is they worship the power of another man. It's like total sexual domination. It's like father worship plus something sexual and creepy. They put on a t-shirt with Che's, Hitler's, Mao's or Lenin's face on it, then they can fantasize about having "personal" relations with father.

A Heathen Family Devotional

Chairman Mao murdered between 60 and 80 million people. Anarchists, go ahead and wear your *"Mao More Than Ever"* t-shirts with pride. Mao captured that harsh individualism that every anarchist dreams of fulfilling.

Chairman Mao was the darkest of fathers. He is worshiped by scumbags around the world. University intellectuals sit in coffee shops and fawn over this mass murderer because he was a 'Agrarian Reformer' who had entire cities executed and buildings bulldozed in order to create more farm land for slaves to work. Mao was a total progressive.

All tyrants believe children should be raised by the state. The easiest way to turn children into mindless minions of the state is to alienate them from their families. Taking children away from home and turning a public school into their surrogate parents is the easiest way to program a child's mind.

In the West today, television, public schools, and consumerism have shattered the traditional family.

The great German Wotanist, Guido Von List said the family is the foundation of civilization. Just by watching the six o'clock news, it's hard to see how anyone could disagree with Von List.

The family is our best protection against tyranny, depression, and social strife. The family is a fortress against the state and money. Having a family and being a traditional parent is a revolutionary act.

A Heathen Family Devotional

Having a family is a blow against the empire.

Tuesday nights should be devoted to the home, motherhood, and indoor chores. Chores create a work ethic in your kids. All kids hate to work, but if you don't make your kids do chores, don't be surprised if they grow up to be lazy bums, living at home into adulthood, or the males end up being metrosexual slackers who have no ambition, never get real jobs, never get married, and buy subscriptions to Gentlemen's Quarterly magazine. A strong work ethic and being a functioning heterosexual man go hand in hand.

Hard work builds moral character in children. When I was around eight or nine, I had a friend who was a Yokut Indian. His father, Cat, worked for the Kern County Land Company. His father lost an arm in a car wreck. He worked for the Land Company feeding as well as watering horses and cattle in addition to fixing the fences. A one-armed man has problems doing this, so his son, Leonard, and I helped him. We used hay-hooks to unload the bales from the flat-bed trucks and to buck the bales up into stacks. We bucked the bales onto his old work pick-up and rode in the back throwing flakes of hay to the livestock. If a fence was down, he told us how to repair it. If a water pipe to a trough busted, he showed us how to repair it.

If I live to be 100, I'll never forget, *"Remember Wyatt, it's left to loosey and righty tighty."* I started working for him in the third or fourth grade, and I stripped a lot of threads (and I mean a lot), but he never got pissed off at me. This is a sign of a great father.

Teach your children, be kind and understanding, never scream and put them down. The whole point of chores is to build up self-confidence in a kid, not to kill his or her ego. Children tend to suck at chores, especially little kids. Many times you have to do more work just cleaning up the mess they made. However, chores are not about getting free slave labor, they are about building character and self-worth in your children. So, never yell at them when they screw up! They are kids after all.

They were poor people and couldn't afford to pay me money for helping them. They fed me lunch and sometimes dinner. However, what they really paid me in was something more important than money. They helped me believe in myself. I wasn't some third grader watching cartoons on a Saturday morning. I was Wyatt the eight-year-old ranch hand. Some kids watched cowboys on TV and dreamed of becoming one. I worked for a cattle company and became a cowboy. Work gives a kid a very different image of him or herself and of the world.

Children have to be industrious, or they may never learn it in adulthood.

Tuesday nights should be devotion to the chores of motherhood.

The free-enterprise system creates a consumer

society. It needs fools to buy, buy, buy! The only morality of capitalism is: *"Owning more crap is good."* This culture is creating a great paradox. The cattle are taught to want more crap. However, we no longer teach a work ethic to children. They are dropped in front of the electric toilet and brainwashed into believing that owning goods defines who they are as human beings. Winners own a bunch of worthless crap and losers don't. The kids are not taught the joy of working. They want things, but don't want to work to get them. It's a *"give me this"* culture. Kids who never had to work, and always get everything for free, grow up into adults who don't want to work and want to get everything for free. We are creating a freeloader citizenship to populate a welfare nation. The problem is the West is de-industrializing. It's becoming poor. It can't afford the social problems it has. It lives on credit. The cattle want free stuff, but hate working. The slacker revolution is coming. It will be a society where shirkers riot because the government can't afford to give them the free stuff they grew accustomed to getting.

Look at the society that consumerism has created. Look at the current riots in Europe. People are rioting because the governments can't afford to give them free stuff anymore. The welfare state creates welfare people.

Both fathers and mothers have to be teachers of a Heathen work ethic.

The free-enterprise system has attacked both the

A Heathen Family Devotional

role of fatherhood and motherhood in the West because mothers and fathers can't afford to buy the newest trendy items. They can't afford new cars, paying $49 a month to watch TV on their cell phones, and all the other rubbish Wall Street sells.

Parents penny-pinch. They have little disposable income. The larger the families, the more parents penny-pinch. This is why Wall Street is at war with the American family. Notice how fatherhood, especially the White father, is belittled on modern TV. Wall Street became a super power after World War Two. The war turned them into global gods.

In the 1940s and 1950s, when most American families had five or six kids, capitalist propaganda endlessly promoted the image of two or three kids with radio and TV shows like Father Knows Best, Leave It To Beaver, The Adventures of Ozzie and Harriet, or the single child I Love Lucy. When I was a kid, living on an oil lease, the average family (for our community) was made up of seven people: two parents and five kids. I had friends who came from thirteen and fourteen member families. How many people today have five or six kids? Most of our people today don't even create families. I can't recall a single radio or TV show when I was growing up that showed the normal large American family. They all showed small families as the new normal. Leave to Beaver was not pro-family. It was an assault on the average large American family. Even the all-American Andy Griffin Show showed tons of adults and one kid, little Opie Taylor. TV's ideal American town, Mayberry, had almost no children,

A Heathen Family Devotional

and this was during the baby-boom!

By the mid-1960s, when the free-enterprise system finally brainwashed the American people to have just two kids, they started promoting the idea of having just one child. When they convinced people to have but one child, Wall Street started pushing no children. When American families stopped having children, then they promoted adopting third world babies and/or homosexuality because homosexuals have loads of disposable cash and no kids.

Democracy wants us to be metrosexual because childless people have more disposable income. The women of the Sex of the City TV show were metrosexual females who were held up as the progressive American ideal and role models for little girls. The cattle were taught to suck oodles of strange cocks and buy a lot of expensive designer clothing...and high-priced shoes, buy lots and lots of designer shoes. The free-enterprise system needs the masses to be metrosexual shopaholics.

Traditional families shop at second-hand stores, plant gardens, sew their own clothing, hunt for bargains, etc. Single childless men and women have money to burn. They don't care about bargains. They don't need to penny-pinch. They are Wall Street's ideal consumer. This is why the free-enterprise system promotes the hell out of the single life and the gay lifestyle. The whole dating culture was created by capitalism in order to train people not to stay in a traditional monogamist relationship. What does capitalism teach you with endless dating, other

A Heathen Family Devotional

than how to end a relationship and move on to the next relationship with your future ex? The death of the family is killing the White race. However, fear not, for the free-enterprise system has an answer for this. They flood the West with Third World immigration to replace the dying White race. Democracy has an answer for everything.

When I was in school, the teachers would often quote Plato, "*What is happening to our young people? They disrespect their elders. They disobey their parents. They ignore the law. They riot in the streets inflamed with wild notions. Their morals are decaying. What is to become of them?*" They did this to mock my parents' generation who were concerned about the amoral television-worshiping baby boomers. The public schools were meant to reassure us that turning our backs on tradition was alright, as well as progressive, and that our parents didn't know anything and were as foolish as Plato. Old people, we were told, have always worried about the younger generation, and things have always worked out. However, things never work themselves out. Read Oswald Spengler's masterpiece the *Decline of the West*. Societies are born, grow old, and die. Civilizations always fall because strong moral people create them and their lazy, worthless progeny kill them. Plato was right. The Greek youth of Plato's day were a bunch of hedonistic pigs who were obsessed with their wanton desires to the point that fucking little boys became the Greek national pastime. Greece was founded by heroes. It was ruled by great families, kings, and republics, until one day, Greece tried democracy and, shortly after that,

A Heathen Family Devotional

Greek civilization died. Ancient Mesopotamia, Egypt, Greece, Rome, and so on were all once great civilizations founded by superb men and women with strong virtues and a splendid work ethic, and they were killed by hedonist pigs who cared about nothing but themselves. Morality matters. Virtues matter. People without morality and virtues destroy civilizations.

Mother should be the principled authority in the home while father is away.

Television and public schools are as immoral as their capitalist masters.

I was in the 4th grade the year they made LSD illegal. It was the same year that President Johnson's anti-drug education program began. We were typical 4th grade boys, thinking about baseball and noticing how girls weren't as gross as they once seemed. We had no idea there was such a thing as marijuana, LSD, reds, whites, nor any other drugs, then one day we were forced by the government to attend drug awareness classes.

We became aware of drugs. Just one minute before our drug awareness class, we had no thoughts on pot, acid, uppers, or downers. After our awareness class, drug use became one of our most popular playground topics. All we boys agreed that we had to find some pot and smoke it. Hip people smoked grass. Our drug awareness class told us so.

A few of us wanted to experiment with LSD and

other drugs. We were eight years old, and the U.S. government had just planted the idea into our brains that recreational drugs were part of our youth culture. Drugs are what we did to rebel against the system; the system told us so.

Youth culture was an idea that the system invented at its universities. No eight-year-old came up with the concept of youth culture. Kids listen to their parents and follow their instructions. The U.S. government was our parents from 7:00 A.M. to 3:30 P.M. The government talked to us between seven and eight hours a day, five days a week. After school, we watched TV for between four and six hours a night. We were lucky to talk to our biological parents for ten minutes a night. The capitalist system truly were our parents. We were the children of the free-enterprise system. Wall Street raised us. We never had a chance.

The system was telling us to rebel against our parents, and the best way to rebel was to smoke dope and drop acid. Our parents surrendered their right of parenthood over to the state. The U.S. government was the true mother and father of our baby-boomer generation, and the nanny state led us to ruin. The public schools were awful parents. They worked to turn my generation against it biological parents and against our heritage and the Western tradition.

Governments are horrible parents. The ten minutes a day my generation had to talk to our parents wasn't enough to undo the capitalist propaganda of

A Heathen Family Devotional

television and public schools. I was lucky that I had more than the average ten minutes talking time with my blood parents, but public school and television were still my moral and intellectual guardian. They guided my generation to do things that profited and empowered Wall Street. They are doing the same thing to your generation.

When I was in the first grade, religion was still required to be taught in public schools. We started class every day with a Christian prayer, a pledge to the American flag and its one nation under God, then Bible study for about thirty minutes to an hour. Bible study was our teacher reading to us from either the Old or New Testament. Back then our governmental parent believed all kids must be Christian, today our state-father changed his mind, and now he is raising our kids to be non-religious. Who knows how the state-father will raise our future children?

Half a century ago, my first grade teacher was reading to us out of the New Testament. She read to us about Jesus. I thought this was a perfect opportunity to apply knowledge I had learned in Sunday school and to prove that I wasn't always just picking boogers and eating them in church; sometimes I actually listened. I thought this was my moment to shine in the sun by kissing my teacher's ass and supporting her with more information on Jesus. She would probably reward me with a gold star on my forehead for being such a helpful little Christian boy.

A Heathen Family Devotional

I stated matter of factly that when the prophet Joseph Smith spoke to Jesus Christ, he said....

Suddenly, someone yanked my arm, pulled me up out of my desk, and shook me violently. My first-grade teacher was shrieking something at me that I didn't understand. She dragged me to the front of the classroom and announced that no one has spoken to Jesus Christ, Joseph Smith was a false prophet and the anti-Christ, and that the Mormon church was in league with the devil. My family was in league with the devil, and my soul was damned to burn eternally in the fires of hell.

It occurred to me at this point that I wouldn't be getting a gold star to place on my forehead.

After denouncing me as the spawn of Satan, she drew a circle on the chalkboard, shoved my nose in it, and made me stand there the rest of the day.

Fifty years ago when I was six, people believed in hell. I grew up in a Christian fundamentalist world where everyone knew (I mean they KNEW!!!) the Bible was the word of God. People believed in Adam, Eve, and the talking snake, Noah's Ark and the Rainbow, Christ walking across water, the anti-Christ, and the forever torture of the fires of hell. Every cell in my body believed sinners suffered fire for eternity. When my first-grade teacher stood me before my class and denounced me as being a cohort of the anti-Christ and of Satan, that was a big fucking deal. Talk about becoming an instant social outcast. No one likes the anti-Christ. He is

A Heathen Family Devotional

terribly lonely.

I am thankful President Kennedy didn't burn witches back then.

The rest of my first-grade year was hell. The things my teacher did to me would be called child abuse today. I never talked about it because back then you didn't talk about things like that. When I was in my early 50s, my youngest brother brought up the subject of how our first-grade teacher would continuously hit him with her hands, shake him, ridicule him in front of the class, and punish him for no reason. That was the first time I ever spoke of it to any member of my family. I never spoke to my parents about it. Hate for Mormons was huge in the 1950s and early '60s. Churches would show anti-Mormon films. It was a lot like the Third Reich showing the Eternal Jew.

My parents paid taxes. They had a right to raise their kids in whatever religion they wished. From the first-grade up to the end of my high school years, I never heard one school teacher say a single good thing about Mormonism. The Christian teachers thought it was a mockery of Christianity, while the liberal teachers thought it was racist and sexist. By the time I was in the second grade, public schools had turned me completely against Mormonism and Christianity. I began to hate Mormonism, and I was pissed off that my parents brought me up in that shit. My thinking was totally the creation of public schools. They turned me into an angry atheist kid. My parents' wishes didn't

A Heathen Family Devotional

mean jack-shit to the government. They were in command of molding young minds. Whether the state swings to the Christian Right or the atheist Left, the minds of our children belong to them. And, we are forced to pay taxes to fund the brainwashing and abuse of our children. Odinism is a minority religion. Minorities always get fucked. This is the ruling law of democracy. The majority fucks the minority. Every Odinist child will become like the outcast Mormon kid of my childhood. Love your Heathen children; keep them the fuck out of public schools.

Public schools are full of little consumers who watch TV, and they HAVE to own the newest horse-shit. The kids who don't own the newest and latest are attacked, mocked, and bullied.

Bankrate shows that a kid costs $190,000 to raise. According to the Visual Economics website at http://www.visualeconomics?.com/wp-content/uploads/20?10/11/kidcosts-FINAL.jpg, they say it costs $222, 000 to raise a kid. I have heard people say it costs up to one million dollars. Why? Because all the shit you have to buy them in order to keep their school friends happy and to fulfill the consumer expectations television filled their heads with. Get rid of the TV and home school your kids, and all that peer-pressure buying propaganda will disappear.

Kids are cheap to raise when you don't have to buy them worthless shit. Most families would be better

A Heathen Family Devotional

off having the mother stay at home, cooking, sewing, teaching, etc. Capitalism promotes working women in order to flood the labor market and to lower overall wage. People didn't need women to work because there weren't women and illegal aliens flooding the labor market and lowering the value of a man's wages. The only reason people today need two paychecks is that women and foreigners have flooded the labor market and lowered the value of real wages. Before capitalism flooded the work market, a father could support his family.

Home schooled kids tend to be better educated than kids who went to public schools.

Public schools are a mess. It's not just the endless consumerism. About 5% of the kids are the "cool" kids and the other 95% are less than " cool." Pretty girls are called "whores" and "bitches", plain girls are " dogs," "fat pigs," and " ugly." There is no reason to hand your kids over to big brother.

Real parents are essential to the well-being of a child. Too many kids today have no real parents. They have television, video games, and the government. Nothing replaces genuine motherhood.

Kids need to help their mother seven days a week. Work is good for the soul.

I love cooking. I bake killer breads. I learned cooking and baking from my mother. She would bake these amazing breads, and the whole house

A Heathen Family Devotional

would smell like a bakery. I know white bread is not the best for you, and we should eat more whole grains, but the smell of white bread fresh out of the oven is like nothing else in the world.

Many families try to create lasting childhood memories in their kids by taking them on expensive vacations to Disney World or Hawaii. However, my best childhood memories are the ones where we just did little everyday things together. Time equals love to a kid.

My mother died a few years ago, and there is nothing that brings her memory back more than baking bread. Every time I bake bread is like I bring my mother back to life. In a way, I do bring her back. Bread is Frey's gift of life.

You can create memories and associations for your kids like my mom did for me.

This isn't a cookbook, but here are a few simple recipes to get you interested in exploring the joys of cooking:

Dutch Dill Rye

Makes four pan loaves or four to ten round loaves.

Ingredients

I am Dutch, German, and British. Our traditional foods have lots of sugar. Young people tend to put in less sugar. You could cut out the brown sugar and use less molasses if it is too sweet for you. Experiment. It will make you a better cook. I like a sweeter rye bread. In addition, if you have no brown sugar, just double the amount of white sugar you use. I think using white sugar, brown sugar, and molasses together gives it a nice kick. I have a huge mixing bowl. If you don't have a giant mixing bowl, just cut all the ingredients in half. If you want to make only one loaf, cut every ingredient by 75%. 5 cups would become 2 ½, and 2 ½ would become 1 ¼. Bread baking is a good time to teach your kids basic math. I went to public schools, so I suck at math.

5 cups of bleached white or whole wheat flour
6 ½ cups rye flour
1 cup lukewarm water
3 cups lukewarm milk
4 packages active dry yeast
4 teaspoon dill weed
3 teaspoon caraway seeds
2 teaspoon salt
1 teaspoon tarragon
2 cup molasses
2 tablespoons white sugar
2 tablespoon brown sugar
4 tablespoons butter

Directions

In a huge bowl, dissolve yeast in one cup of lukewarm water. I am an old fart. I check the water temperature the old fashioned way by sticking my finger in the water. If you start to scream and cry, the warm is too damn hot. It can't be so hot it kills the yeast. Most cook books say 110 degrees, but I have always just used my finger.

Add wet ingredients to mixing bowl first, then dry ingredients.

Next, use a mixer to blend the yeast water mixture, molasses, butter, milk, sugar, caraway seeds, tarragon, salt, and 2 cups of rye flour. Mix every-thing well. Next, add the remaining rye flour and mix it completely. Once the rye flour is all mixed in, add the wheat flour and mix it until you can knead the bread.

Knead the bread for about 10 to 15 minutes. If the dough is messy, add more wheat flour until it is dry enough to knead. After you are done kneading the bread, cover it with a cheese cloth or whatever you use. Let the dough rise for one to two hours or until it doubles in size.

Beat the dough down. This is the part I like best about baking bread. I feel more manly in my apron when I punch out the dough. Punch the dough down, divided into four pan loaves or four to ten round loaves. Grease the loaf pans or the flat baking sheets (I use two pizza pans) for the round loaves. Let the dough rise again for about two hours or until it doubles in size.

Preheat the oven until it gets to 375 degrees F, then

A Heathen Family Devotional

at 375 bake the bread for 30 to 35 minutes.

Pigs in a Blanket

This is most likely the first thing I ever cooked. I remember making this when I was really young, possibly between 2 and 3 years old and got biscuit dough in my hair and up my nose. Hey, I was a kid. It's a kid's job to make a mess. I loved making these when I was little. First, sit your kids down at the kitchen table, put a plate in front of them. Place a frankfurter on the plate. Open a package of refrigerated biscuit dough. Place a piece of biscuit dough on each one of your kids' plates. Teach your kids how to wrap the dough around the frankfurter. It doesn't have to be perfect. They're kids. They make mistakes. It's all part of learning. Cooking with your kids is to teach them self-esteem and that working is good and rewarding. Don't put your kids down for making mistakes. Place the Pigs in a Blanket on a greased cookie sheet and bake at 350 degrees for 10 to 15 minutes. Pigs in a Blanket are great with mustard.

Cheesy Pigs in a Blanket

This is very popular. Many people wrap a slice of American processed cheese around a hot dog before they wrap around the biscuit dough. However, I found this is a problem when you have little kids making Pigs in a Blanket because they almost always tear the dough and the cheese just melts onto the cookie sheet. Here is a kid-friendly method

A Heathen Family Devotional

of making Pigs in a Blanket. Take a greased bread pan, then have your kids fill the bottom of the pan with a bed of refrigerated biscuit dough. This method will use two package rolls of biscuits. Once you have made a bed of biscuits, have your kids use a butter knife to cut an eight-pack of frankfurters into small pieces, then have the kids spread slices of hot dog to cover the biscuit bed. Once the franks are spread to cover the bed, cover the franks with grated parmesan, cedar, mozzarella, or jack cheese. After you have covered the franks with cheese, take a second roll of biscuit dough and cover the franks and cheese. Bake at 350 degrees for 12 to 18 minutes.

Pizza Bread

This is for kids three or four on up. It's easy and fun. My mother taught me how to make it when I was four. It builds up a kid's self-esteem. I taught my friend's kids how to make pizza bread when they were really young. The parents would never cook; they always ate out or ordered fast food. So, whenever they came to my place, the kids would constantly nag me to let them make pizza bread. I got to where I would always have the ingredients for pizza bread around my place in case the family would show up.

Ingredients

Makes one slice of pizza bread

You can use any ingredients you normally use on a

A Heathen Family Devotional

pizza. I used to have mushrooms, crooked sausages, bell pepper, and so on out for the kids, but they always went for these standard ingredients. In addition, I have tried many types of bread, but I always found that a good, firm, sliced sourdough bread works the best for pizza bread.

One slice of firm sourdough bread.
One jar of spaghetti sauce.
Grated parmesan, cedar, mozzarella, or jack cheese. I like using all four cheeses.
One package of thinly sliced pepperoni.

Directions

Get your kids and sit them down at the kitchen table. Put a plate in front of them and give them a spoon. Put a slice of sourdough bread on the plate. Have your kids take the spoon and spread spaghetti sauce on one side of the bread for the pizza sauce. Next, have them cover the pizza with thin slices of pepperoni, then top it all off with cheese. Like I said, you can use other ingredients like mushrooms, ham, chicken, cooked hamburger, bacon, onions, tomatoes, olives, and so on, but I found most kids love a simple pepperoni pizza. Put the pizza bread on an un-greased cookie sheet. Cook at 300 degrees F for 5 minutes. Fun kid lunch.

Pizza Potato Skins

This is an alternative to Pizza Bread. Take some potatoes and bake or microwave them until they are done. Cut the potatoes in half. Take a spoon and scoop out the guts. Leave enough of the potato "meat" to support the skins. Put the guts of the potatoes in the fridge for tomorrow. The potato guts can be served the next day. You can add cheese, broccoli, and a little butter. Microwave them until the broccoli is cooked and have a good kid lunch. Once you gut the potatoes, let your kids fill the potato shell with spaghetti sauce, parmesan, cedar, mozzarella, and/or jack cheese, as well as pepperoni, mushrooms, ham, cooked chicken, cooked hamburger, bacon, onions, tomatoes, olives, and so on. Put the potatoes on an un-greased cookie sheet. Heat oven to 400 degrees and bake for 10 to 15 minutes.

Home-cooked food is very spiritual and Folkish. Fast food is the food of Wall Street, and Wall Street is the devil.

Household chores are important. Good spirits such as house-wights, kin-fetches, etc. are attracted to clean homes and repelled by dirty homes. Bad spirits are attracted to dirty homes and repelled by clean ones. Happy homes attract good, and sad homes attract bad. Work makes kids into good people. Lack of work turns kids into monsters.

Here is a prayer of thanks for house work.

"Hail Odin, God of Fatherhood. Hail Frigga, Goddess of Motherhood.

Thank you for blessing me with this time I can spend working with my family.

A Heathen Family Devotional

Hail Frigga, Goddess of the Home.

Thank you for giving me the health and ability to do housework, and thank you for bringing my family closer together through chores.

Hail Kin-Fetch, my ancestral guardian.

Thank you for helping me make my house a home.

Hail House Wights, the Spirits of this house.

Thank you for giving this home life.

Hail Frey, the Spirit of the Field.

Thank you for our daily bread.

Hail the Green Man, the Spirit of Life.

Thank you for making the plants grow.

Hail Eartha, the Spirit of this planet.

Thank you for giving my food a place to live.

Hail all Gods and Goddesses. Hail all Wights. Hail all Aelfin. Hail all my ancestors. Hail all creatures big and small who bless and protect our home and who help us in our daily chores.

As a small offering of thanks, I give you this (name the offering). Hail all known and unknown forces of

A Heathen Family Devotional

the Divine.

> *Alu, Alu, Alu.*
> *Alu, Alu, Alu.*
> *Alu, Alu, Alu.*

A Heathen Family Devotional

Chapter Thirteen

Wednesday is Family Government Night

"One of the penalties for refusing to participate in politics is that you end up being governed by your inferiors."

Plato

"Among (the Icelanders) there is no king, but only law."

Adam of Bremen 11th century C.E.

"Each of the wise should wield his power in moderation; He will find that no one is foremost when bold men gather.

The Havamal

The only way Heathenism can stop being a mythology study group and become a mature religion is through prayer and active contact with Our Living Gods.

A Heathen Family Devotional

Likewise, the only way we can get the Western business world to serve Our People and Our Gods is if our Heathen families move into the business world in the Age of Man and position ourselves so that we can take back the Western economy for the coming Age of the Gods.

Even if you are working-class and can never start a business of your own, teach your children and grandchildren to be business people or other professions of power like military leaders, law makers, law enforcement, teachers, journalists, religious and political leaders, bloggers, authors, craftsmen, and so on.

The Age of the Gods will only come when Heathen families build a bridge between Our Folk and Our Gods.

The West is turning to crap because the people in power are crap. Their philosophy is crap.

Business must be guided by a moral hand.

Adam Smith, the so called father of capitalism, believed that gluttonous rich people don't need to be moral and concerned for their workers because through "an invisible hand" prosperity will trickle down on the poor.

In his book, *The Wealth of Nations,* Adam Smith wrote, *"...he intends only his own security; and by directing that industry in such a manner as its produce may be of the greatest value, he intends*

A Heathen Family Devotional

only his own gain, and he is in this, as in many other cases, led by an invisible hand to promote an end which was no part of his intention. Nor is it always the worse for the society that it was not part of it. By pursuing his own interest he frequently promotes that of the society more effectually than when he really intends to promote it."

The "invisible hand" doesn't work because it doesn't exist. Trickle-down economics is just as big of a hoax as socialism. Government hacks can't run an economy just as economies can't run themselves. We don't need an invisible hand, but a visible one. We need the hands of moral, decent people to guide the Western economy. This is where you come in.

All Odinists must work to create their own corporate family that will be one of the guiding hands that move the West. The corporate family must be built on Folkish, pro-Western values. The corporate family must become the guardian of our people. The corporate family must become the Divine bridge between Our Folk and Our Gods. The corporate family must become the visible hands of Our Gods on earth.

You must teach your children and grandchildren to become leaders and lead justly, kindly, and to serve Our Folk and Our Gods. The corporate family should not be motivated by greed as the free-enterprise system is, but on service to Our Folk and Our Gods. The West is in the mess it is in today because it has mixed the teachings of Adam Smith and Karl Marx together to create the Philosophy Of

A Heathen Family Devotional

The New World Order. This international materialism is spiritually dead and is killing the earth and our people.

The West is falling apart. The Left blames it on the Right, and the Right blames it on the Left as the cowards in the middle try to figure out where the new Center is located so they can safely hide behind it.

The Left, the Right, and the Center are the problem, not the answer.

The world's economic problems are bigger than the political hacks claim. The West is de-industrializing at the same time the free-enterprise system is flooding our labor markets with cheap labor from the third world.

Our wealth, which took over 12,000 years to create, is being murdered by international profits.

The wealth of the West is like an old-growth redwood forest that took millenniums to grow, and one day, Wall Street came along and convinced the masses to let them clear-cut all the redwood trees and sell the wood to Communist China.

Wall Street promised our people clearing the old-growth forest would create jobs, and it did at first, until Wall Street realized that they could bring in third world labor to do the work cheaper. As our people sat idly by, watching the redwood trees disappear, the smarter ones realize the promised prosperity never came.

A Heathen Family Devotional

One day all the redwoods were gone, and they would take millenniums to grow back. Wall Street took the profits it made from selling off our wealth and vanished. Our people were left in a West emptied of all of its wealth. The Third worlders, inside our homeland, were taught by television and public schools that our people are the devil behind all their problems, so they declared war on us for giving them a West with no wealth. This is the future democracy and the free-enterprise system are bringing us. It's already begun.

Wall Street is the enemy of our people. They don't care about us. They care only about profit.

The Marxists think profits are bad. Odinism does not. Profits and wealth are good if they serve the people. The government needs to protect its own people. The free-enterprise system believes only in profits. There is no "our people" in free enterprise. Global profits are all that matter. Obama didn't create this mess; Adam Smith and Karl Marx did. Both were anti-nationalists and saw nationalism as a problem.

Both labor and business must serve the nation. The nation must protect its own labor and its own business. If not, the nation will die.

Internationalism is being sold to us by the Reds and the Neo-conservatives (Neo-Cons). America was always a protectionist nation until recently. Now America promotes the global village, world without borders, world democracy, the socialist international, a New World Order, and this universalistic crap. Internationalism is killing America.

The internationalist propaganda is endless. We get it from TV, schools, and all the other arms of the New World Order.

The New World Order hates patriotism and nationalism. However, they are never afraid to wave an American flag in the faces of the dense when they need to control them. When Wall Street wants to make war profits, all it has to do is wave an American flag in the faces of the cattle, and they will support the wars and send their sons.

It's amazing what the cattle will believe. The big lie that "American wealth turning into international profits and leaving America to build factories overseas is good for America" is something only a fool would believe, but most Americans believe wealth leaving our people is beneficial because the international capitalists told them it was. In reality, it kills our wealth to send it away. It doesn't make us richer. How on earth could it?

Western wealth, moved to the third world by international banks to build slave factories there, has never trickled down and helped the working class in the West. This is the big lie of free enterprise. Nothing ever trickles down on the workers' heads but acid rain and poop from birds.

Nations and people become wealthy because noble-

A Heathen Family Devotional

men and women took it upon themselves to protect the wealth of the nation and its people.

The answer to the dying Western economy isn't totalitarian socialism nor the free-enterprise system distributing our wealth to the third world, but returning to the old ways of family corporations.

There has always been evil in the world. Some people and some families are just no good. Equality is a myth. No two people are the same. Man is a herd animal. Inequality is how herd animals operate. In human societies there will always be alphas, betas, and omegas. There will always be outsiders who are your friends, and insiders who are your enemies. There will always be people who betray their own kind. This is the history of mankind, and it will never change because we were created to be this way.

Family corporations are natural because families are instinctive herd units. Governments like the Medieval Catholic church, communism, Nazism, and so on always ended up employing mass murder to herd the cattle because they go against the natural family organization, and when ever you go against human nature, violence happens.

Families are a passive way to organize people. Healthy families are good, kind, and helpful. Normal people love their families. It's better to organize people in units they love than using the Iron Heel.

There are many dysfunctional families, but they are

A Heathen Family Devotional

not the Folkish ideal.

Healthy families are the only perfect organization mankind has ever created. Families have been able to do things that neither socialism nor capitalism have ever done; they can create a perfect world to live in.

Chris Donnellan is a long-standing friend of mine, who I have known since the old days of the Los Angeles Odinist Fellowship in the early 1980s. Here is a story he wrote about his father and the old American way of doing business. Americanism and the Norman Rockwell America of my childhood has been murdered by capitalism.

Here is Chris' story:

"My father came out to California from New York when he was 18, in 1959. He just got out of high school and wanted to get away from NYC and his overbearing Irish Catholic Mother. As soon as he arrived, he obtained a job in a Printing Plant just east of Los Angeles. It was a family-owned business and unionized, except that management, workers, and the owners all worked together and took care of one another for the good of the company. In fact, it was more like a big extended family than a business. My Father stayed there for almost 40 years. By the end of his career, the original owner and founder died, and his heirs sold out to the first corporation which made an offer. The corporation came in and destroyed the union by telling the workers that either the union had to go, along with

A Heathen Family Devotional

mandatory $7-10 pay cuts for all workers, sharply reduced benefits and pensions, or the plant would be closed down, and operations moved overseas. My father was heartbroken by this and soon developed cancer afterwards. A few years later, after the workers made all the concessions the new corporate owners demanded, they closed the plant anyway and moved operations to Mexico. This is how the system changed in just 40 years or so."

The man who created the Printing Plant where Chris' father worked was a very Folkish man. He was part of mother nature's natural nobility. He was a Jarl without ever knowing what a Jarl was. He was a noble leader who served his people and made sure they got the money and health care they needed to support their families. This is true Americanism, and the true nature of the Jarldom: Noble people being noble to serve the Folk. This man was a true son of Odin, regardless of whatever religion he may or may not have practiced.

Chris' father's life came to an end when his Jarl died and was replaced by demonic termites from the ice pits of Hel, or as we call them in America, the free enterprisers. Business men and women with no morality other than money are just as bad as the Marxist pinheads. They both are killing the West.

Here's my father's story:

My grandfather, Tunis Kaldenberg, lost the family farm because drought hit the year before and he, and many other farmers in the area, didn't have the

A Heathen Family Devotional

money to buy seeds for next year's crops. They asked the President of the United States for help and to loan them the money to buy seeds. The President told them he deeply believed in the invisible hand of the free-enterprise system and that those who were too weak to survive must be allowed to fail. Of course, the international capitalists who helped pay for the President's election campaign were simply too big to fail, and the President had to help them any way he could for the good of the nation, but small family farmers didn't donate large sums of money to elect the leaders. Therefore, family farms were just the right size to fail. The invisible hand of the free enterprise can be brutal if you don't have the money to buy politicians.

After my grandfather lost his farm, he somehow got his hands on some exotic animals and the Kaldenberg family owned a small traveling circus that didn't do well. By 1928, my grandfather crawled up into a bottle and disappeared. My dad was 12 then. My grandfather and his children from another marriage left the circus animals with my dad and his mother. They didn't give them any help. My dad dropped out of the 7th grade to take care of his mother and the circus animals. He worked on a newspaper route. He worked on a horse-drawn ice wagon delivering blocks of ice house to house. He worked at a feed store. My dad worked all the time to support his mother and his animals. He never had much of a childhood. He fought in World War II in order to make the world safe for Wall Street.

In the 1920s and '30s, the oil fields where I grew up

A Heathen Family Devotional

had a very violent history. This made the unions fairly strong, and violence helped improve the lot of the working class. Violence is the visible hand of the working class. Sometimes it's the only hand they have. If America didn't have a violent labor history, we would never have had much of a middle class.

In the 1950s, my father got a job with Standard Oil. They promised him a good retirement plan. My dad worked all his life and had little free time, so he took the job with Standard Oil because the idea of retiring appealed to him. He was an ideal employee. He seldom missed a day of work. A good company would take care of a man like that.

By the 1980s, during the Reagan years, Adam Smith's invisible hand theory became known as the trickle-down theory. Illegal aliens and women were starting to flood the labor market, and the law of supply and demand was pushing down true wages. The union stopped being violent and became weak.

One day in the 1980s, my father was close to retirement age. He could smell that retirement money Standard had promised him in the 1950s. However, something was wrong with Standard Oil. My father had noticed that the bosses had called in every single worker near retirement age to the office and offered them a promotion into middle management. EVERY ONE OF THEM. My dad smelled something fishy was going on. He turned down the promotion. His bosses were pissed at him. Every single one of the workers who accepted the promotion into middle management got fired and lost all their retirement benefits, because the unions didn't protect middle management. The workers complained to the unions. However, since the unions were no longer run by working-class people, but by upper class liberals with university degrees, what were they going to do? Suck the cocks of the capitalists extra hard and make them cry? It's not like a rich liberal would ever pick up a gun and do something.

After Standard Oil fired all the workers who got promoted to middle management, the company came after my father. My father went to the unions for help, but what would liberals who have university degrees do? Write a strongly worded letter? The unions are a joke because they are run by jokes. Without violence to back up their words, the unions are nothing.

Standard Oil bullied my father into early retirement, and they gave him a " package deal." What a deal it was... for Standard Oil, a handful of cash instead of his promised pension.

I was told a story that one of the men, who accepted the Standard Oil promotion into middle management and lost everything, became despondent. He rented a room in a motel where the invisible hand of the free-enterprise system placed a gun in his mouth, pulled the trigger, and splattered cherry pie all over the motel wall. God bless Adam Smith.

American family businesses tend to care about American workers, and international capitalism doesn't give a shit about us. Families are people,

A Heathen Family Devotional

and people can be both good or bad. Conglomerations aren't human. They are just things. They have no heart. They have no soul. Is having heartless, soulless things running our economy wise?

Charles Dickens' *A Christmas Carol* is a great yuletide movie for Heathen families. I know it's a traditional Christian movie. However, it is full of Odinic morality: the importance of family, spirits, and how bad morality can affect your entire life. Ebenezer Scrooge and Jacob Marley are two miserable businessmen who have screwed up their Wyrd. The three spirits of Ghost of Christmas Past, Ghost of Christmas Present, and the Ghost of Christmas Yet to Come remind me a lot of the three Wyrd sisters at Yule. Old Fezziwig and his family are like old-time Jarls: The Lord and Lady of the House who take great care of their people. The Fezziwigs are like ideal kindred leaders. They kept the spirit of Yule alive and gave Ebenezer Scrooge some of his best youthful memories. Fezziwig is the exact opposite of what Scrooge grew or warped into.

Ebenezer Scrooge is Adam Smith's ideal business man. Smith promoted all that "greed is good" crap. Smith believed that profits from the greedy help the poor by building workhouses. Dickens was NOT a socialist. He never said the state should take over all businesses, but businesses must be good, kind, and serve the Folk as well as the nation, like an extended family. Charles Dickens was very nationalistic and revolutionary. Businesses are to serve the nation and the people, not the greedy pigs like Scrooge.

A Heathen Family Devotional

Adam Smith believed protectionism was dreadful. Profits are an end in themselves: Business and labor DO NOT serve the nation and the people; they only serve money. Utopia will grow out of unchained profits. Nations are in the way of profits. The poor are uplifted by the rich pissing on their heads. The trickle-down theory is that an invisible hand will hold the rich man's penis as he blesses the working class in a golden shower. Smith's ideas created much of the cruelty in capitalism and caused 12,000 years of Western wealth to be moved to Red China and elsewhere.

We need blood over gold, not piss covering the working class. Business must serve our people, not destroy them. Our people come before gold.

Profits and wealth are beneficial if they serve the people. The government needs to protect its own people. The free-enterprise system believes only in profits.

Odinists must create corporate families that run like a business that works for the well-being of our people. Odinists must become the enlightened hands that guide our people along their way. If we don't become, as the Christians say, the good shepherd who leads his flock, then the devil will take our place and lead them for us, as he is now doing.

When I was young and my parents were active in the Church, Wednesday nights were family government night. We would meet as a family and talk about problems with others inside and outside of the family, personal problems, family finances, vacation plans, family chores, allowances, and so on. For a while, my parents tried to run our family like a democracy, but five kids voting against two adults on how to spend the family money ran into problems quickly. I, for one, always voted we should spend the family money, not for food, clothing, nor other practical items, but to pay for trips to Disneyland. Who needs food and clothing when you're at Disneyland? At age four or five, I wasn't afraid to run around Tom Sawyer's Island buck naked.

Democracy is an awful system of government. Morality and justice can't be determined by simple numbers. Five kids voting against their two parents will destroy their household. The parents will have no voice. Two parents voting against one kid is just a dictatorship where the kid can never win. There is nothing magical nor fair about democracy. It's simple math. Six rapists voting on what to do with your teenage daughter can never lead to justice.

Family government is an idea that works well with Odinism, and Wednesday is the perfect night. Wednesday, Wōdnesdæg, or Woden's day comes from the Anglo-Saxon's Day of Odin/Woden. Odin is the King of our Gods. He is the God of leadership. Family government is about teaching your kids how to become leaders. Odinists are the chosen people of Odin. It is your duty as an Odinist to lead and influence other people. Odinists must become the Jarldom of the coming Age of the Gods. We have to train our children and grandchildren for the things that are coming. The Age of Man is dying. Our progeny have been chosen to lead the future.

Democracy teaches your kids that number counting (the majority has a right and duty to dictate its will over a minority) creates nothing but very screwed governments because the majority of the human race are imbeciles. Why should 50 morons have the right to dictate their idiocy to 20 geniuses? Are numbers the source of all morality? Why should 10 rapists have a right to rape your daughter? Fuck the majority. When have the masses ever been right about anything? A drunken mob whipped up by a demagogue to lynch an innocent man is the purest form of democracy on earth. That's total power to the people, and the people are usually wrong.

Good is good, and bad is bad. Good doesn't need a show of hands to be good. Likewise, bad has the power to be bad regardless of what the cattle herd thinks. Good and evil exists separately from the mass-mind. The masses have no influence over good and evil, and most of the time they couldn't recognize morality if it grabbed them by the ass.

My parents tried family democracy and, like democracy always does, the five people who had no money got to vote on how they would spend the money of the two people that had some. Family democracy meant we could spend our parents' money until the household was in trouble just like all Western democracies are doing today.

A Heathen Family Devotional

You know rich people have few kids. Perhaps Odinists should get on welfare and have lots of kids and vote on how the industrious people will spend their money. We should vote that they spend it all on us by increasing our welfare benefits, so we can have more babies who can grow up and vote on how to spend productive people's money. I am half-way joking, but there are many groups of people in this society that are doing just that. Democracy is the coward's way of re-distributing wealth.

I think Odinic family governments should be based on the old system known by some as Thingism. The pre-Christian Germanic people didn't practice democracy. They were governed by assemblies where noble men voiced their opinions and tried to influence the leadership. There was no voting at all. A Jarl from each group was allowed to attend a Thing. He was accompanied by three Karls, who acted as Oath Helpers. The Things were forums for the opinions of the Jarls. The only power the Jarls had was influencing the king, the chieftain, the gothi, the law speaker, or whoever.

Democracy only teaches your kids the art of bullying. Thingism teaches your kids the art of persuasion.

All Odinists should be free to choose any form of government they wish to run their family by, be it anarchy, communism, fascism, democracy, or whatever.

However, I think Thingism is the best. This is how it

works.

The father and mother are the Lord and Lady of the house. They have all the power. On Wednesday night, you hold family meeting to create the rules of the household, to assign chores, to air family grievances, to create family budgets, to grant weekly allowances, and so on.

This is better than democracy, communism, fascism, anarchy, and so on. It teaches your kids how to promote themselves, how to debate issues, how to persuade others and influence them to do what they want.

Thingism teaches your kids that they are an active member of your family. They can and should learn how to sway family politics in order that they can learn how to manipulate the outside world and not have it manipulate them. Family government teaches your kids not only that they are part of your family, but it also gives them the skills to leave, go into the outlander world, and to create and run a family of their own. Look at all the 40-year-old TV watchers who still live at home with their mommy and daddy because their parents never taught them how to be dominatant leaders eager to leave home and conquer the outside world.

Too many people today don't know how to create and follow a family budget. They live from paycheck to paycheck, which means they are always broke, living off of credit, and in debt to international capitalism. Family government night is when you

A Heathen Family Devotional

should work out the family budget with your kids. They are never too young to learn about money.

Wednesday Family government night is when you should teach your kids the art of being noble and ruling Odinism in the Age of Man and into the coming Return of Our Living Gods. Odinism needs leaders, and this is where your children, grandchildren, and the rest of your progeny come in.

48 Rules of Power, by Robert Greene, is a book every Odinist father should read to his children at bedtime. *Power: Why Some People Have It and Others Don't,* by Jeffrey Pfeffer, is also a wonderful for reading to your kids. *Managing With Power: Politics and Influence in Organizations* is another superb book, by Jeffrey Pfeffer, to teach your children how to become Jarls and Erins. *Influence: The Psychology of Persuasion,* by Robert Cialdini, is excellent for teaching your kids the art of Thingism. These books will do more good for your children than reading that meaningless *Cat in the Hat* book to them.

The coming world must be ruled by an Odinic meritocracy, not a democracy. The best Odinic people must be pushed to the top of society while the worst people must be taught how to toil.

All Odinic families were chosen by Odin to lead our people out of the darkness. This is our Wyrd. Teach your children to fulfill their destiny.

Foremost in leadership is money, since it's easier to lead with money than without.

A Heathen Family Devotional

Most adults today know nothing about practical finances, so the great thing in teaching your kids about money is that you may learn something too.

Here are some other good books for teaching your kids how to lead:

The No-Cash Allowance: A Practical Guide for Teaching Your Children How to Manage Money, by Lynne Finch. This book won the Mom's Choice Award. Lynne Finch has created a financial system that starts with three-year olds. Her system teaches kids money management. She has a program to teach youngsters the relationship between services and income. Finch includes many kid-friendly charts, graphs, and other visual aids. This works well with Odinism. We must teach our kids the value of work. They live in your home and must do chores to help pay for their room and board, clothing, medical bills, and so on. They can't be freeloaders. They have to work if they want to live in your household. If they want an allowance, they have to do extra work in addition to the chores they all ready do. Unless, of course, you want a lazy, pot smoking 50-year-old man sleeping on your sofa the day you die because the turd never learned the value of work and has no idea how to manage money. If you don't teach you kids the value of work and money, who will? The public schools? Ha!

Rich Dad, Poor Dad for Teens: The Secrets About Money--that You Don't Learn in School!, by Robert Kiyosaki. This is a great book for teens. All the

A Heathen Family Devotional

books in this series are high-quality.

Rich Dad's Rich Kid, Smart Kid: Giving Your Children a Financial Headstart, by Robert Kiyosaki and Sharon L. Lechter. *Rich Dad's Rich Kid, Smart Kid* teaches kids how to organize their lives to become successful. This book contains a guide for helping to build up self-confidence in kids. One of the best things in this book is the authors teach kids about the de-industrializing of the West. How working for companies no longer will guarantee job security or even a job, for that matter. Capitalism is moving our jobs to the third world and flooding our Western labor market with cheap third world labor. The working class is fucked in the West, and things will never get any better without radical change.

Blue-collar jobs are dead. America and the entire West now has an information and service economy. This is where the future money will be. I disagree a little with these books. I do believe unskilled labor is screwed, but craftsmanship will always have a place. We are told of the new rules of the new economy and how everyone must prepare to be a free agent. In other words, if you don't get smart and make yourself rich, you will be bouncing from job to job like a temp worker. Companies are no longer loyal to their workers. He makes the point that school is pretty useless because everyone (he claims) must retrain every two to four years or change their careers because it's the latest thing for companies to layoff people they think have been in a position "too long." In the old days, companies believed it was wise to keep older employees on the

A Heathen Family Devotional

job they knew. Today, the business world teaches that old employees are a burden to a company and new employees bring in fresh blood and fresh ideas. Younger employees get sick less, and you can layoff old people and not pay them a retirement like Standard Oil did with my father. Capitalism grows more heartless.

Rich Dad's Rich Kid, Smart Kid is terrific for homeschoolers. The book introduces the reader to the teaching methods of Howard Gardner, an American developmental psychologist who is a professor at Harvard University. He is famous for his theory of multiple intelligences. He believes we learn eight different ways:

1. Spatial is visualizing a picture of the information in your mind. When you wish to recall the information, you bring the image backup. I do this a lot.

2. Linguistic is learning from words such as reading, writing, listening to lectures, and talking. Lectures tend to bore me, but I learn a lot from writing, talking, and reading.

3. Logical-mathematical is learning through numbers, logic, scrutinizing, and reasoning. I learn through abstractions and investigating, but I don't have a mathematical mind at all. This is too robotic for me.

4. Bodily-kinesthetic is learning through movement of one's own body or watching others move. Many athletes, actors, doctors, law enforcement, military,

and professional criminals are bodily-kinesthetic learners. This theory is what got me interested in Howard Gardner. In college, I studied with a friend who played college basketball. When he was sitting still, he had a very hard time learning. However, pacing back and forth in his dorm room, waving his hands in the air and talking out loud sometimes nearly shouting, he could learn almost anything. He was a total bodily-kinesthetic learner. I have to sit perfectly still to learn. Moving around is just a distraction.

5. Musical is learning through sound. These people often sing songs in their head or rhythm things. The famous Alphabet song, " A, B, C, D, E, F, G...." is possibly the only thing I have learned musically. In my book, *Odinism: The Religion of Our Germanic Ancestors In the Modern World*, the Australian Odinist, Osred, stated that he creates rituals by singing them. I can't do that. I have to write them down and re-read them nine times in order to remember them. People's minds work very differently.

6. Interpersonal is learning as you relate with other people. These people are usually very social and learn best intermingling with others. This isn't me at all. I use to hate it when teachers made us do group projects together.

7. Intrapersonal is learning when you think by yourself and have no input from teachers or other students. This is totally me. I enjoy learning alone. I never could pay attention to a teacher standing in

front of a class and talking. I normally would read something that interested me, or I would look out the window and daydream.

8. Naturalistic is learning by watching the world around you. Naturalistic learners tend not to learn from books, but from living. I am a huge naturalist learner. I believe the best way to learn about Our Living Gods is by natural learning. Listen to the Gods and study the nature.

Mr. Gardner teaches that each child learns and expresses knowledge differently. His method is to find out how a child understands and employs information, then reinforce that child with public admiration. Once you appreciate how a child learns, build your lessons around their natural learning habits.

Raising Money Smart Kids: What They Need to Know about Money and How to Tell Them, by Janet Bodnar. This book has a lot of common sense advice on how parents should teach kids about money. There is a great quiz for parents that will force you to question your relationship with your kids and money. The book has a list of questions that kids ask about money and the author gives you a list of answers that might work for you.

Growing Money: A Complete Investing Guide for Kids, by Gail Karlitz, and *A Kid's Guide to Stock Market Investing,* by Tamra Orr, are two first-rate books for kids on how to invest in the stock market.

Most of the books in the Berenstain Bears collection

A Heathen Family Devotional

are useful. They have few words and lots of pictures. They are splendid for opening up a dialogue with your kids about numerous topics. Read them first. If you dislike some of the things they say, just add your own text and use the art as a teaching aid. Some of the text is Christian, so be warned. Here are some of the books I like:

The Berenstain Bears' Trouble with Money, The Berenstain Bears' Dollars and Sense, The Berenstain Bears and the Trouble with Chores, The Berenstain Bears and the Homework Hassle, The Berenstain Bears Get in a Fight, The Berenstain Bears and the Bad Influence, The Berenstain Bears and the Trouble With Friends, The Berenstain Bears and a Job Well Done, The Berenstain Bears and the In-Crowd, The Berenstain Bears and the Messy Room, The Berenstain Bears and the Gift of Courage,The Berenstain Bears Show Some Respect, The Berenstain Bears and Too Much TV, The Berenstain Bears and *Too Much Junk Food.* These books claims to be for 4 to 8 year olds, but I think they are better for 2 to 4 year olds.

These are just some ideas for Wednesday's family government meetings. The point of this night is to teach your kids that they are part of your family and that the workings of the family is their business, too. Talk with them, be truthful, and let them know what's going on with the daily affair of your family. People who keep their kids in the dark just alienate them and weaken their family. Strong families talk often. Dysfunctional families never talk; they just fight.

A Heathen Family Devotional

Here is a prayer for family government.

"Hail Odin, the Father of Our Heavenly House. Hail Frigga, the Mother of Our Heavenly House.

We thank you for watching over our home and for giving us a guiding hand. You give us the wisdom to govern our family. Without your love and leadership, our family would be lost.

Hail Thor, the Heavenly Protector.

We thank you for protecting our home and our family. Without your watchful eyes, our lives would be less secure.

Hail Tyr, the God of Power.

We thank you for empowering us with the courage to lead ourselves and others. Without you, we would be enthralled by tyrants.

Hail our Kin-Fetch, the Other Mother of our family.

We thank you for being the spiritual "Mother's Little Helper" of our household. Without you, this house would be less governable.

Hail our House Wights, the Spiritual Lords of our Manor.

We thank you for being the Other Fathers of our family. Without you, this house would be less

A Heathen Family Devotional

governable.

Hail all who help this family govern itself. Without you, this house would be less manageable.

As thanks for all that you blessed this family with, we make this offering of (name offering).

Alu, Alu, Alu.
Alu, Alu, Alu.
Alu, Alu, Alu.

A Heathen Family Devotional

Chapter Fourteen

Thursday is Family Game Night

"If your children spend most of their time in other people's houses, you're lucky; if they all congregate at your house, you're blessed."

Mignon McLaughlin,
The Second Neurotic's Notebook

As a kid, I loved family game night. It was lots of fun, and I got to talk to my parents and my siblings. We use to play lots of games. We would have a family game night almost every night. We played Monopoly, Carrom, Dominoes, Parcheesi, Sorry! Chinese Checkers, Clue, Masterpiece, Battleship, Old Maid, Go Fish, and so on. I hated Boogle, Scrabble, and other word games. When Uno and Skip-Bo came out, my parents were instantly addicted. I remember when I used to go to friends' houses for a sleepover, and they never had family game nights. They didn't do anything together. They just sat in the living room and stared at the television. No one would utter a single word. They just sat peering into the light of the boob tube like zombies.

When kids would come over to my house for sleepovers, they had a blast. They got to do things they didn't get to do at their own home. My friends would always tell me I was lucky to have such cool parents, and I was remarkably blessed to have such parents.

How loving of you to make your own children so lucky.

None of us can control what kind of government we live under nor what is going on in the outside world. However, all of us can control what happens inside our own homes. Heathens must turn their homes into a child's paradise.

Game night will make you the cool parents in the neighborhood.

Buying games normally cost under $20. If you take care of them, they last forever. By turning off the TV and focusing your kids' minds on games and family fun, you're not only making your family tighter, but also, you're taking your kids' minds off of TV commercials. This could save you 10s of 1,000s of dollars from all the crap you no longer have to buy your children because the television is off.

Supposedly, my generation only talked with their parents on the average of ten minutes a day. The

A Heathen Family Devotional

baby-boomers were the first generation where their parents dropped them down in front of the television and used this Wall Street propaganda machine as a baby sitter. I spoke to my parents a lot more than ten minutes a day. However, life is short. Childhood is even shorter. I lost a lot of precious time watching TV. This time could have been better spent talking with my folks. They are dead now, but the television lives on spewing out Wall Street vomit and trying to convince me that I am a failure in life if I don't buy the latest "hot item." Do you really want your kids believing they are failures if they don't own the newest "hot item" the international capitalists are selling?

It's hard enough being a kid without having television filling their minds with self-hating bullshit.

Love your children, turn off the tube, and get out the old Parcheesi board game. It helps build a stronger family. It saves you money since your kids aren't being pounded to death with Wall Street's message of "Buy! Buy! Buy!," and games are fun.

Here's a prayer for Thursday family game night. As I said in other books, "Alu" is the holiest word in the Odinist religion. It literally means ale or beer. Those damn Krauts and their beer! Alu is a holy word, perhaps, because ale or beer was the standard thing to offer the Divine during rituals, and it just evolved as a sacred word connecting the Gods with the Folk. However, this is just a guess. No history of why Alu is a holy word has survived.

A Heathen Family Devotional

"Hail Odin, the Great Father. Hail Frigga, the Great Mother.

Thank you for helping us bring our family closer together.

Hail Thor the Great Brother, the jolliest of the Gods.

Thank you for bringing into our household the joy and laughter of games and sportsmanship.

Hail Frey and Freyja, the brother and sister of pleasure.

Thank you for bringing happiness and delight into our home.

Hail our Kin-fetch, the Spiritual Matriarch of our home.

Thank you for weaving the web that brings this family closer.

Hail our House Wights, the Spiritual Patriarch of our home.

Thank you for bringing the power of fatherhood into this house and empowering us to lead our own lives.

Hail to all Gods, Goddesses, Aelfin, fetches, wights, and all other ancestral spirits that help make this a joyous and happy home.

A Heathen Family Devotional

As thanks for all you do for this household, we offer you this gift (name offering).

Alu, Alu, Alu.
Alu, Alu, Alu.
Alu, Alu, Alu.

A Heathen Family Devotional

Chapter Fifteen

Friday is Family Fun Night

"Each day of our lives we make deposits in the memory banks of our children."

Charles R. Swindoll,
The Strong Family

Family activities bring your family closer together, and it gives you more time to converse with your kids. There are lots of great family activities you can do for little or no money.

Friday family fun night can consist of either home activities or a family night out.

Home activities can be a game night. It's Friday night and a good time to allow your kids to have a friend or two sleep over. Game night is a lot more fun for your kids if they have a friend over. However, be careful, for many times other people's kids are little monsters.

Friday nights can be a special dinner your kids help

A Heathen Family Devotional

to cook. Television sucks, but if you don't have cable or a TV antenna and just have a DVD player, television can be used for family movie night. Rent a kid's movie and make a ton of popcorn. Since you don't allow your kids (ideally) to zombie out in front of the idiot box, Friday movie night could be a special event. Maybe do it once or twice a month. It's a hell of a lot cheaper than going to the movies.

Friday nights could also be arts and crafts night. Maybe you could rotate movie night with arts and crafts Fridays. Public libraries have lots of free books you can borrow on arts and crafts. Disney's Family Fun magazine has some really neat arts and crafts kids can do. It's Disney, so they are always pushing to sell something to make a buck. So, be cautious of the avaricious Disney leech. Disney is a profit-driven monster.

Friday nights are fantastic for family outings. You can go to the movies, although they cost a fortune. If other Odinists live near, ask them if they want to come along. You can reinforce a sense of community in your children by having them socialize with other Odinic families. It's good to have your kids befriend other Odinist kids. Besides, if you go to the movies with single Odinists, you can con them into buying your kids popcorn and soda. The popcorn costs more than the price of a kid's ticket nowdays.

Drive-ins are a thing of the past. I am lucky. I live down the street from a great drive-in. It's by the beach. I love going in the winter on foggy nights and watching horror movies. My folks used to take us to drive-ins a lot because it is cheaper. You save on popcorn and drinks. They would make a huge bag of popcorn, have a cooler full of drinks, and bring candy. We didn't have a pick-up truck or a station wagon, so my parents brought lawn chairs so we kids could sit outside and watch the movies. If you are lucky enough to live near a drive-in, use it.

About eight times a year in California, we get terrific meteor showers. Taking your kids for a "shooting star" watch is wonderful. I like the August falling star event the best because summer nights are pleasant and cloud free. I have satellite radio in my car. They have one channel that has nothing but programs from the golden age of radio. They have excellent science fiction shows like X Minus One, Escape, Inner Sanctum Mysteries, Arch Oboler's Plays, The Weird Circle, westerns like Gunsmoke, Have Gun, Will Travel, Frontier Town, suspense, detective, action, and adventure shows like Box 13, Suspense, Sam Spade, Lux Radio Theatre, Tarzan, Superman, The Shadow, Pat Novak For Hire, and comedies like the Bob Hope Show, Phil Harris & Alice Faye, Burns & Allen, Jack Benny Program, Amos and Andy, Red Skelton Show, and many more.

The cool thing about radio is, unlike TV, you can do other stuff as you enjoy the shows. You don't have to sit like a zombie and watch the radio. Moreover, kids enjoy many of the shows. It's great for star watching. The meteor showers only come eight times a year, so it's not really a Friday night activity unless you are lucky. However, you can star watch

A Heathen Family Devotional

most Friday nights, at least in the summer. Learn astronomy with your kids, buy them a telescope, go out into the night, and identify constellations and planets. You can buy a cheap portable BBQ for under $30, fill it up with wood and roast hot dogs or make S'Mores under the stars. Out in a lovely summer night, roasting marshmallows to make S'Mores, listening to one of Arch Oboler's scary plays, as you watch for falling stars is a perfect family night.

Friday night walks are enjoyable. You can walk around town or do a nature walk. Fairly decent night-vision binoculars can be bought for under $400. They are great for spotting birds, rabbits, coyotes, and so on in the dark. Alternatively, you can sit up on a hill with your kids and see what types of wildlife they can identify.

Going on a Friday night family drive can be nice. You can have a destination or just explore the world. Driving in the car is a useful time to talk to the whole family about Odinism. Don't be afraid if you can't answer some of the questions your kids ask about the Gods. You don't have to know everything. No one knows everything except Frigga, but she is keeping her knowledge to herself. Therefore, we can never have all the answers. The important thing is that you and your family learn about the Divine together.

The main thing about family fun night is to do something fun as a family. Talk to your kids, connect with them, make your family stronger, and make yourself a stronger Heathen.

A Heathen Family Devotional

Here is a prayer for Friday Family Fun Night

"Hail Odin, Paterfamilias and holder of the house.

Hail Frigga, holder of the keys.

We thank you both for holding our home together.

Hail Thor, the life of the party.

We thank you for good company.

Hail Heimdall, Lord of Divine Bridges.

We thank you for helping bridge our family to together.

Hail Freyja, patron and protector of the Folk.

We thank you for watching over us as we let our guard down in times of joy.

Hail Bragi, the patron of entertainment.

We thank you for enriching our souls.

Hail our Kin-Fetch and House Wights, who sentinel us.

We thank you for your devotion to this family.

Hail all who help us on this night of family fun.

A Heathen Family Devotional

As a show of gratitude, we offer you (name the gift).

Alu, alu, alu.
Alu, alu, alu.
Alu, alu, alu.

A Heathen Family Devotional

Chapter Sixteen

Saturday is Family Adventure Day

"Kids spell love T-I-M-E."

> John Crudele, American writer

Saturdays, my parents often took us on day trips. They would wake us up early in the morning (4 am to 6 am, depending on where we were going) and carry us half asleep to the car where we fell asleep again only to re-awake hours later in places like Morro Bay, San Francisco, San Diego, the Los Angeles Zoo, Disneyland, and so on. They would have a whole trip planned out.

At the end of the day, often we returned in the wee hours of the night. We kids sleeping all the way home. It was cool. We took these long day trips, but were allowed to sleep through the long boring ride. They made for great childhood memories, and they brought our family closer together.

You don't have to take such long trips. You can take

local trips to explore the countryside or a nearby town.

Saturday could be arts and crafts day, or you could have your kids assist you in building something or working on a car. In bigger communities, they have arts and crafts fairs that are free. This could help you find a hobby they enjoy. Become a boy or girl scout leader. The scouts have many great activities, and as their den leader you could do lots of interesting things with your kids. The scouts allow dens to pick their own religion. I knew a family that had an Asatru boy scout den. This would work for people with a fair sized local Heathen community.

Here are three national chains that offer free workshops for kids.

Michael's offers free events and workshops for both adults and kids. Here's how to contact them:
http://www.michaels.com/Projects/projects.default.sc.html

I took the munchkins to some free jewel classes, painting classes, and pottery classes. They do these free classes in hopes of getting you hooked just like a dope dealer giving out free samples of heroin. However, if your kids get hooked on pottery, 50 pounds of clay only cost around $23. And believe me, 50 pounds of clay will last a six-year-old a long time. Firing pottery is cheap. Low Fire is only $1.25 for a two-inch piece, while a fourteen-inch piece is just $4.00. Why would you have your kids making a giant fourteen-inch piece? High Fire Glaze is just

A Heathen Family Devotional

50c to a buck more per piece. You can get a cheap glaze kit that comes with brushes and numerous colors for under $30. As long as you don't let your kids go hog wild with the glaze it should last you awhile. Save money by just having your kids paint runes, Thor's hammers, and other religious symbols on the pottery.

Lowe's has some great workshops for kids. In San Diego, they have these classes every Saturday at 10:00 am. This website implies that they only have wood projects for kids, but the Lowe's nearest me has lots of gardening classes for kids. Here is their pitch: https://www.lowesbuildandgrow.com/

"From project basics to giving your child the opportunity to say, "I built it!", our Build and Grow kid's clinics are a great way to help build confidence! Bring the kids into any Lowe's store and build a FREE wooden project. Each participant also receives a free apron, goggles, a project themed patch, and a certification of merit upon completion of their project."

Building up your kid's self-esteem is what it's all about.

The Home Depot's Kids Workshops are free for kids ages five to twelve. Held on the first Saturday each month at every store.

http://www.homedepot.com/webapp/wcs/stores/servlet/ContentView?pn=Kids_Workshops&langId=-1&storeId=10051&catalogId=10053&cm_mmc=thd_mar

A Heathen Family Devotional

keting-_-digitas-_-hic_site-_-kidsworkshops

Here is their pitch:

"The Home Depot's Kids Workshops offer useful projects including the creation of toolboxes, fire trucks and mail organizers, as well as more educational projects, such as a window birdhouse, bughouse or Declaration of Independence frame kit.

The workshops teach children do-it-yourself skills and tool safety, while at the same time helping to instill a sense of accomplishment. Additionally, this fun time allows for quality one-on-one time between adults and children.

In addition to the newly constructed project kit, each child receives a kid-sized orange apron, similar to The Home Depot associates' aprons, and an achievement pin."

The Creation Station is a chain that is only in the United Kingdom. This is too bad because it's the coolest kids arts and crafts shop. The whole store is built around kids.
http://www.thecreationstation.co.uk/

Here's their pitch:

"You can probably tell but we are PASSIONATE about nurturing creativity!

We love having fun with different materials, paint, glue and of course, a little bit of glitter. We believe

A Heathen Family Devotional

being creative is about experimenting, playing and just seeing what happens. Having a go and being creative in a social environment provides so many benefits;

From making choices, sharing, listening, observing, playing, pretending, problem solving, interacting with others, to mention just a few.

This is not about learning to paint a horse, but it is all about having a go, being inspired by something quite simple and encouraging each person's own ideas to see what happens. There is a huge boost of confidence when ones own ideas are taken seriously and acknowledged, no matter what age you are.

We hope you find these pages inspiring and that we can help to inspire your child's own journey of discovery and a love of learning."

How cool is that? The entire store is devoted to building up your kid's self-esteem through arts and crafts. I'd trade a hundred American Wal-Mart stores in order to have one Creation Station in the United States. Hell, if Creation Station did come to America, Wall Street would figure out a way to turn it into something evil.

All of these chain stores have it right. Arts and Crafts, gardening, wood projects, household chores, etc. built up a child's self-worth. Kids who believe in themselves grow up into successful adults. Kids with low self-esteem become unsuccessful adults with a low sense of worth. Do you really want your

A Heathen Family Devotional

kids to grow up to be self-hating losers? If not, find chores and hobbies that they can succeed at. Little successes truly matter in building up a kid's self-worth. If you find something that a kid isn't good at, move on until you can find something they can do. Never yell at your kids or tell them they are stupid. Little kids look up to their parents like they are gods. When "God" tells a kid that he or she is a "little dumb fucker", the words echoes through the kid's psyche sometimes for a lifetime. Do you really want that? Words matter to children, especially when they come from their parents. Be careful. Be kind.

Saturdays are also a great time to meet with other Odinists in the area. When I was a member of the Odinist Fellowship in the 1980s, Sigi Harrbard rented a large house in Woodland Hills to be a Hof (an Odinist temple). As far as I know, it was the first Odinic temple in North America and perhaps the first one since the Third Reich closed all the Heathen temples in Germany in the 1930s. Our Hof was open 24/7. Sigi wanted Wednesday Nights to be the great gathering, but Saturday turned out to be the day most people came. This is when most people are off of work, and Sunday was never as popular of a day for people to come because of football on TV, some members were married to Christians and had to go to church, and lots of people just like to kick back at home on Sundays before the Monday workweek begins. So, Saturday is a great time for Odinic meetings.

You can take your family and meet Odinist friends

A Heathen Family Devotional

at the park for a picnic, or you can just do picnics as a family. The Odinist Fellowship often had camp-outs starting Friday evening and ending at noon on Sunday. Some people would show up Friday evening and stay through Sunday afternoon, while others would just come up for Saturday and leave that same night. Camp-outs are great bonding time with your kids, and they can have fun with other Odinists. We sometimes had people come to our camp-outs as far away as Europe and Canada just to meet other Odinists. The Heathen world was much smaller back then, and people would travel far just to feel they were part of the Odinic community. Odinists and Asatru groups are all over the West now and there is always something local going on, so people tend not to travel as much as they did in the beginning of modern Heathendom. Why should people in Germany fly to California when today German Heathens have enough people to have their own camp-outs?

Focus on your family. Odinism is a family-based religion. It has to grow out of your family. Odinism is a Folkish movement, which means it grows out of the people's connection with the Gods, and it is not a Universalist movement that grows out of a single leader's "wisdom" like Christianity grew out of the teachings of Jesus Christ, Islam grew out of the teachings of Muhammad, Communism grew out of the teachings of Karl Marx, National Socialism grew out of the teachings of Adolf Hitler, and so. All these Universalist cults are inorganic and come from demagogues and not from the Folk.

A Heathen Family Devotional

Folkish religions come from the people. They don't come from leaders. Folkish means "from the people." If you are part of the people, then Odinism comes from you. You can learn from reading what other Odinists say and think. However, our religion lives in our blood. Therefore, you are like the Vatican City of Odinism, and we are all the Popes.

Here is a prayer for Saturday family adventure.

"Hail Odin, the Great Wanderer

We thank you for seeing us safely on our journey.

Hail Frigga, the Goddess of Common Sense.

We thank you for filling our family with common sense, so we can travel safely.

Hail Thor, Lord of the Good Life.

We thank you for making our family adventures fun and safe.

Hail Bil, the Weaver Goddess.

We thank you for helping up weave this family together.

Hail Heimdall, the Great Watchman of our Gods and of our Folk.

We thank you for watching over our family as we seek escapade.

A Heathen Family Devotional

Hail Njord, Lord of Travel.

We thank you for watching over this family as we journey to find adventure.

Hail our Kin-Fetch, who is this family's personal protector.

We thank you for traveling with us as we seek adventure.

Hail all who protect this family as they travel.

As an offering, we give (name the gift).

Alu, Alu, Alu.
Alu, Alu, Alu.
Alu, Alu, Alu.

A Heathen Family Devotional

Chapter Seventeen

Blood Matters

"You don't really understand human nature unless you know why a child on a merry-go-round will wave at his parents every time around - and why his parents will always wave back."

William D. Tammeus
Columnist for *The Kansas City Star*

I don't mean to write this to hurt anyone's feelings. There are many fine Heathen families that are made up of adopted children, foster kids, and step-children. They are very good and loving families. However, mother nature created special ties that no other family except a biological family can ever experience. I know this isn't Politically Correct. It doesn't support the system's agenda to re-define the meaning of family. I know many of the mindless cattle will be upset that anyone challenges the thoughts their masters planted inside the herd's jellied brains. However, biology is a fact of life. Genetics connect living creatures. No matter what TV and your Marxist public school teacher tried to beat into your head, blood matters. Families tied together by blood have a special relationship like no other.

We live in a culture of ballyhoo and hoaxes, where heroes are demonized, and scum bags are turned into "gods." This is the great trickster society where lies are held up as truths and truths are mocked as lies. This is Loki's land where, the people are controlled by hedonism, greed, and deception in order to bring about the fall of our people and our civilization. The Great Trickster brings forth Ragnarok, the death of our multi-verse.

Tricks and lies are a bad thing. When people are devoted to a trickster, they are devoted to a con-artist, a hoaxer, and a liar. Why is this a good thing? Even the Great Trickster, Coyote, in Southern California Indian lore was never seen as the good guy. Coyote was the Deceiver, the Con-man, the Fool. Eagle was the noble one, the good one.

The Age of Man is Loki's time. The coming Age of the Gods is Odin's time. Ragnarok is the death of this multi-verse and the rebirth of another in its place. When Ragnarok comes, this multi-verse will die in a Big Bang that will create a brand new multi-verse as it has countless times before, and as it will countless times again into infinity.

Always question every idea this Age of Man promotes, because Loki, the Trickster, is behind this culture. Every idea of the Age of Man was created to harm our Folk and Mother Earth. Even the most innocent sounding ideas of this culture are

A Heathen Family Devotional

a trick to promote Hel's agenda.

Hel is Loki's daughter, the Goddess of death, sickness, and the Age of Man. This Death culture has declared war on our families. Be careful when Death tries to re-define the meaning of family. The bitch is always up to something no good.

Natural families are made up of people who will always be connected for the simple truth that they have the same blood. An ounce of blood is worth more than a pound of friendship. Adopted families, foster families, and step families may love one another, but blood relations stick together even when they hate one another. I have known many adopted families, foster families, and step families that were connected when they loved each other. Their love made them loyal. However, I never met one that were still loyal to each other once the love died. Most blood families I know remain loyal to the black sheep of their family no matter how disgraceful they behave because they are *STILL* family. They are still blood. Blood matters. Blood is thicker than water, as the old saying goes.

My grandfather Kaldenberg was a poor excuse of a man. He poisoned his blood by drinking Loki's piss, until it became his life. I will never forgive him for abandoning my grandmother and father when they needed him the most. However, he is my blood. I have offered prayer to the Gods for his soul. I don't want him to spend eternity in Hel's pit, nor do I want him to join Loki's army at Ragnarok (the death of this multi-verse). I pray to the Gods to lift up my

A Heathen Family Devotional

grandfather's soul and bring it into Asgard with the rest of his ancestors. I do this only because he is my blood. If this piece of shit was just my step-grandfather, his ass could stay in the fucking Abyss forever, as far as I care.

Not every blood family that hates each other is loyal, but the only times I have ever seen families that deeply dislike one another and still stayed loyal are families that are blood related. My grandfather and grandmother Kaldenberg are a perfect example of how blood relationships work. When my grandfather Kaldenberg became a drunk and left his wife, his children from a previous marriage became disconnected with my grandmother, even though she was the woman who raised them and my grandfather was never there for any of his kids.

They sided with my grandfather, even though he was a worthless scumbag drunk who abandoned my grandmother. They only did this because my grandfather was their blood while my grandmother was not. They were all adults with money by the time my grandfather abandoned my grandmother for good, but none of them helped her out with even a penny. My father dropped out of school at the age of 12 in order to get a job to help support his mother because she was blood. Blood is thicker than water.

Blood matters. This is not politically correct, but it is the truth. Nothing is closer than people bound by blood. No divorce can ever truly divide a family based on blood. Your blood kin will always be your blood kin. However, step-families, adopted families, in-laws, and marriage partners can walk out of your life for little to no reason. Blood is important because blood is forever. Water comes and goes with the tide.

This is not saying that adopted families, foster families, in-laws, and step families can't be close. Many are very close, but they can never have the magical union of blood.

My mother's third step-father was half-French and half-Blackfoot Indian. He was no blood-relation to me at all. Both my blood grandfathers died in the Great Depression long before I was born. However, Felix LaClair, my grandmother's fourth husband, was a decent man and treated my grandmother well. I loved him for that. He was born in the 1800s like all of my grandparents, and he died before I became an Odinist. Regardless, I wrote and read a prayer for his soul. I made it to both his Blackfoot and French ancestors. I don't know what happens to racially-mixed people after they die, since more than one set of ancestors is calling them home to join them in a different afterlife. Sean and I talked about this when we headed the Heathen Folk Revival. We both came to the conclusion that the souls of racially mixed people will split into separate pieces with each piece returning to its proper ancestors. Therefore, half my step-grandfather's soul went to Asgard to be with his French ancestors, while the other half of his soul went to live with his Blackfoot ancestors in their own happy hunting grounds.

A Heathen Family Devotional

My grandmother's second husband, my mother's first step-father, was a cruel drunk who used to beat my mother and abuse her. He beat her so bad that he broke most the teeth out of her jaw on one side of her face. This prick's name was Arthur. When my mother turned seventeen, World War II started and she joined the Navy as a member of the W.A.V.E.S. (Women Accepted for Volunteer Emergency Service). She did this to escape Arthur.

I prayed for my step-grandfather, Felix, because he was a good man and had earned a prayer. I didn't pray for my step-grandfather Arthur because he belongs in Hel's pit. I prayed for my real grandfather because he was blood. If my step-grandfather, Felix, would have been a worthless piece of shit like my grandfather Kaldenberg or my step-grandfather Arthur, I would never have prayed for him. I love my grandfather Kaldenberg because he is blood. Outside of that, the shirker had nothing going for him. Blood matters. This is not a Politically-Correct statement, but it is the truth.

Blood families are more forgiving to one another. Blood relatives can get away with murder, but non-blood can not.

If you are not blood related to your family, you can do things to win their love and respect, but don't be surprised if they don't treat you equally to blood family, because you are not. Most people do this sub-consciously and have no idea they are doing it because it's instinctual to put blood above water.

A Heathen Family Devotional

It's a basic survival instinct that has evolved over four billion years, and all the politically correct social engineers can never change human instinct no matter how much Marxist bullshit they heap on the cattle. The human instinct of "blood protects blood" isn't going away anytime soon.

Nevertheless, whether you are a family bound together by blood or not, family activities can help bring you closer.

Many Heathens cite the Norse practice of fostering as an example of adoption. However, normally an uncle, the father's brother, would foster his nephew. Sometimes it would be the mother's brother, but the uncles were always blood related. Blood matters.

A Heathen Family Devotional

Chapter Eighteen

The Final Thoughts

"The voice of parents is the voice of Gods, for to their children they are heaven's lieutenants."

William Shakespeare

The West is in a mess. No government of the Left, Right, or Center will save us. We are the only answer to our problems. Our families are the answer. As George Bernard Shaw said, *"... the greatest social service that can be rendered by anybody to this country and to mankind is to bring up a family."* Creating a strong Heathen family will do more good for the West than a million marches, political speeches, or elections. Family matters, which is why most tyrants in history have feared the family.

The National Socialists taught German children in Hitler Youth to inform on their parents. The Communists taught Cambodian children to beat to death their parents with shovels and ax handles. Wall Street used television and the music industry to teach White children to rebel against their parents in the phony "Generation Gap" of the 1960s.

A Heathen Family Devotional

Evil works to turn children against their parents.

The family is the brightest light of civilization. It is the bedrock of our Folk. Our families are good. The system is bad.

The Heathen family is a state within the state. We can't overthrow this system. We can't even have any influence over it. The beast does as it wishes. It lies and uses propaganda that claims, "the people are in power." However, their tricks and lies only fool dullards. Thinking folks know the people don't control this system. Money controls it. International money has all the power. Nonetheless, we can create some power for ourselves. We can create a government that we control and that works for our best interests. This government is the Heathen family.

We can build Heathen families with little to no money. If need be, we can get on welfare and let the damn system support our families. If capitalism has flooded the labor market so severely in your area that your lowered wages can't support your family, then fuck the system! Drop out of the workforce and let capitalism support your family. Don't kill your children just so you can make it in the capitalist world. If the pigs make things so unbearable, let the pigs support you and your family. Welfare can be a revolutionary act. Suck the public teat dry. What good is the system? It doesn't have the best interests of our people at heart, so fuck the system. Bleed the devil dry. The system hates our people, then hate it back. Never let this pig society murder your family. Kill the system first. This isn't our society. The faster it falls, the sooner we will get our own nation. The Age of the Gods will not come until the Age of Man falls. So, burn, baby, burn! Get on unemployment, disability, food stamps, whatever free money you can get to support your family and drain the beast. What good has this system ever done for us? Not a damn thing.

Create a Heathen family by any means necessary. If this means getting a job, then get a job. If this means getting on welfare, then get on welfare. If this means robbing a bank, then rob a bank. Family is everything. Family is the future. Family is the greatest temple to our Gods you can ever build. Without family, our people die. Without our people, our Gods die. We are biologically connected to our Gods. They are of our blood. We are of their blood. We are kin. Odin is our Father both spiritually and biologically. We are the children of Odin. Our family is HIS family.

Be patriotic to your family, not to a government that wishes to destroy your family. The problems of the West are no accident. They have been planned from long ago. The system is not your friend. It is your enemy. They know it. You should know it.

The West is run by Loki's brood. These Lokians rule the Age of Man. They will have to fall before the Age of our Gods can replace them. In the meantime, create your Heathen family. Make your family strong. Create family wealth, but if you can't create your own wealth, then suck the wealth out of the Lokian system. They plundered it from our people

A Heathen Family Devotional

anyway. The wealth of the West belongs to us, not them.

Devote yourself to our Gods. Pray to our Gods. Make offerings to our Gods.

The Age of Man feeds off the spiritually dead. It brings Ragnarok closer. Prayer makes the Divine stronger. The more we pray to the living Gods and devote ourselves to them, the more we push back Ragnarok, weaken the Age of Man, and bring forth a resurgence of the Age of Gods.

The Light of the New Dawn illuminates as Ostara raises her head.

We Odinists have to save ourselves by building, advancing, and promoting Odinic families. If you are someone who has no Heathen children, chances are you have extra cash. Instead of becoming a metrosexual, going to the mall, and blowing your free cash on the latest crap Wall Street wishes to sell you, find a good Heathen family that wants to have more Heathen children, but can't afford them. Help the Folk by becoming the reborn Uncle Ebenezer Scrooge and keep the spirit of Yule alive seven days a week. If the struggling Heathen family wants more kids, but can't afford them, become the sponsor of their family and help lift the financial burden from their shoulders. Raising Heathen children is a community affair. If for whatever reason you can't have kids, help someone who can.

CPSIA information can be obtained at www.ICGtesting.com
Printed in the USA
LVOW011630301011